Winning Your Wife Back

Before It's Too Late

Winning Your Wife Back

Before It's Too Late

A Game Plan
for Reconciling
Your Marriage

Gary
Smalley

Dr. Greg Smalley
Deborah Smalley

THOMAS NELSON PUBLISHERS®
Nashville

Published in Nashville, Tennessee, by Thomas Nelson, Inc.

Scripture quotations noted NKJV are from THE NEW KING JAMES VERSION. Copyright © 1979, 1980, 1982, Thomas Nelson, Inc., Publishers.

Scripture quotations noted NIV are from the HOLY BIBLE: NEW INTERNATIONAL VERSION®. Copyright © 1973, 1978, 1984 by International Bible Society. Used by permission of Zondervan Publishing House. All rights reserved.

Scripture quotations noted TLB are from *The Living Bible*, copyright © 1971. Used by permission of Tyndale House Publishers, Inc., Wheaton, Illinois 60189. All rights reserved.

Scripture quotations noted PHILLIPS are from J. B. Phillips: THE NEW TESTAMENT IN ENGLISH, Revised Edition. Copyright © J. B. Phillips 1958, 1960, 1972. Used by permission of Macmillan Publishing Co., Inc.

Scripture quotations noted NASB are from the NEW AMERICAN STANDARD BIBLE®, Copyright © The Lockman Foundation 1960, 1962, 1963, 1968, 1971, 1972, 1973, 1975, 1977. Used by permission.

Library of Congress Cataloging-in-Publication Data

Smalley, Gary.
   Winning your wife back : a game plan for reconciling your marriage / Gary Smalley, Greg Smalley, and Deborah Smalley.
   p. cm.
   Includes Bibliographical references.
   ISBN 0-7852-7045-0 (HC)
   ISBN 0-7852-6028-5 (SC)
   1. Husbands—Religious life. 2. Marriage—Religious aspects—Christianity. 3. Reconciliation—Religious aspects—Christianity. I. Smalley, Greg. II. Smalley, Deborah. III. Title.
BV4528.2.S53 1999
248.8'44—dc21
                                         99-20326

Printed in the United States of America

06 07 RRD 5

Contents

*To Norma, who for thirty-four years has been my best friend, com-
panion, lover, and encourager. Thank you for winning me back.—
Gary*

*To the three people who remind me daily of what matters most in
marriage and in life: Erin, Taylor and Madalyn
With all my love—Greg*

*With profound gratitude these pages are dedicated to my awesome
parents, Frank and Audrey Smalley, whose 53-year marriage beautifully demonstrates their strong commitment to God, their family,
and each other.—Deborah*

Acknowledgments

This book represents the contributions of many people who struggle to better understand marriage and to help married couples. First and foremost, we acknowledge our friend, mentor, and colleague Dr. Gary Oliver, who has provided much wisdom and insight, both personally and professionally over the years.

We also deeply appreciate the talents and support of Terry Brown and the staff at Smalley Relationship Center. Thank you Jim and Suzette Brawner, Jimmy Funderburk, Roger Gibson, Sheila Green, Debbie Meyer, John Nettleton, Michael Smalley, Norma Smalley, Sheila Smethers, Lori Vanderpool, and Terri Woolsey.

We would like to express our deep sense of appreciation for the individuals and couples who have shared their lives and marital journey with us. We would like to thank them for allowing us to share their personal journey of marital reconciliation.

We thank Mike Hyatt for his enthusiasm in developing this project. We also thank Cindy Blades and the staff at Thomas Nelson for their support and expertise during this process.

Most important, we thank the Lord for his blessings and for making so many things plainly evident for our learning and growth.

Introduction

The foundation of all relationships is honor. Fulfilling marriages must be built upon that foundation. All of us long for a strong and close-knit marriage that will last a lifetime. But often we have not applied the knowledge and the skills of how to honor or love our wives.

Some of you who read this book are ready to give up and start all over. We believe that there is hope. Changes do not happen overnight. It will take work and consistency. All great things in life require commitment and dedication.

We believe your wife is worthy of your complete dedication to love and honor her. No matter what your marriage scoreboard reads or how bad your marriage seems, you can make a decision to love her with all your heart and soul.

As you begin this book, ask God to create a clean heart that will honor and love your wife back into your life. God bless your journey!

Gary Smalley

Pregame . . . .
Warm-Up . . . .

Lord, I Need a Miracle!

Winning your wife back may seem like a long shot, but the game of life often provides us with examples brimming with hope.

In many minds the game was all but over. The fat lady hadn't started singing, but she was definitely warming up! On January 3, 1993, the NFL's Buffalo Bills and Houston Oilers were locked in a fierce battle of extreme importance. The winners would advance in the play-offs while the losers would be given plane tickets home and the season would be over.

Houston jumped out to an early 28–3 half-time lead. The Oilers played an almost flawless first half, making the Bills look like an amateur team. It didn't look good for Buffalo, down by so many points. As the Bills regrouped in their locker room at half time, their coach, Marv Levy, no doubt reminded his team that the game wasn't over. He most likely urged them not to panic. Sure, changes needed to be made— and fast. The offense wasn't scoring, and the defense was allowing too much of it. In just minutes, the Bills' locker room turned into a classroom, and everyone paid attention.

In this crash course, the players probably heard lectures like these: "Let's identify our mistakes and make the necessary adjustments . . . We've got to execute better in the second half . . . Remember what got us here!"

Methodically and patiently, teams have come back from being touchdowns behind. But turning this game around would take nothing short of a miracle.

The Rout Continues . . .

The second half had barely begun when Houston intercepted a Buffalo pass and returned it for a touchdown. The scoreboard revealed a horrible sight for Buffalo fans: HOUSTON 35, BUFFALO 3. Fans booed. TVs clicked off. It was officially a rout.

Never before had an NFL team come back to win from a 32-point deficit. For those who decided to stay tuned, the very next possession saw Buffalo do something it hadn't been able to do all afternoon—sustain a drive. Six minutes into the third quarter, the Bills marched the ball down the field for their first touchdown. The score was a little more respectable: HOUSTON 35, BUFFALO 10. The Bills quickly set up for an onside kick, and when the players were unstacked, Buffalo had possession! The momentum that had once belonged to Houston was making its way to the other sideline.

No Las Vegas oddsmaker could have predicted what happened next. In that historic third quarter, Buffalo scored four touchdowns in less than seven minutes, and the Bills went ahead 38–35! However, with twelve seconds left in the game,

Houston tied the score on a 26-yard field goal. Unbelievably, the game headed into sudden-death overtime. The first team to score would win!

Houston won the coin toss, and it appeared that Buffalo's valiant effort would fall short. But Houston quickly turned the ball over on another interception. Miraculously, three plays later, the Bills kicked the winning field goal and completed the single greatest come-from-behind victory in NFL history! Final score: BUFFALO 41, HOUSTON 38.

Developing a Game Plan

What an unbelievable game! But you may be wondering what one historic football game has to do with winning your wife back. Everything! Perhaps you are staring at your marriage scoreboard, and it doesn't look good. You realize it will take nothing less than a miracle to win back your wife and kids. You long for a comeback, another chance. If you identify with this situation, we encourage you to realize that the secret for reconciliation is illustrated by something that happened during the Buffalo game. That's right. The secret for winning your wife back is really just an elaborate version of what the Bills' Coach Levy undoubtedly told his players at half time:

Don't panic. Let's take a good look at our mistakes and make the needed changes and adjustments. We must realize that there is no way to get it all back with just one play. But if we can sustain a drive and give it all we've got, there is no limit to what we can accomplish. Now get out there and win!

As the Buffalo players raced back onto the field, you could sense something was different. In the first half, Houston's quick lead so shocked the Bills that they couldn't recover in order to execute their game plan. It was as if they were playing at night and someone had turned off the stadium lights. Because of the darkness, the players lost perspective and started running around aimlessly. And before they knew it, they were down by 25 points. But during the second half—as the result of rediscovering their game plan—the lights came back on and they remembered how to win.

When your wife walked out the door, your confusion perhaps felt like that of the Hollywood celebrity who went with his friend to a retirement home. While his friend visited with his father, the celebrity waited out in the lobby. He hadn't been sitting for very long when an older woman started talking to him. The woman laughed and told stories for about an hour. Finally, it dawned on the man that she might not recognize him. So he gently asked, "Ma'am, do you know who I am?"

"No," she politely answered, "but if you go to the front desk, they'll tell you."

Depending on when your wife left (or asked you to), you might be able to relate to this man's confusion. At times, the chaos and disorder of your situation can make you feel like asking someone at the front desk, "Please tell me who I am."

Like men playing football in the dark, you can't seem to find the light switch, although you've tried many things. You may be wondering what will happen to your family, your friends, and your life. Over and over again you ask yourself, What now? What should I do?

When the Buffalo Bills needed a miraculous comeback, they had to go into the locker room and rediscover their game plan. In the same way, one of the greatest things you can do at this moment is to develop a clear and specific plan of action. You need a step-by-step plan, or the opposing team (the marital breakup) will continue to pound you in the dark. We invite you to discover the secret to winning your wife back.

Pregame Warm-Up

When his team was down by 25 points, Buffalo's Coach Levy didn't know what the score would read once the clock ran out, but he wisely altered his game plan to maximize his team's chances of winning. He knew that what they had been doing wasn't working and that they had absolutely nothing to lose by trying something new. He was like a painter who worked for a wealthy woman with a valuable antique vase. The woman was so fond of the vase that she decided to have her bedroom painted the same color. Several painters tried to match the shade, but none came close enough to satisfy the eccentric woman.

Eventually, a painter showed up who guaranteed that he could match the color. After several days behind closed doors, the painter finally revealed his work. The woman was so pleased with his work that the news spread around town and the painter became rich and famous.

Years later, the painter gave the business to his son and retired. But before the father left for Florida, his son asked him a very important question. "Dad," said the son, "there's something I've got to know. How did you get those walls to match that vase so perfectly when no one else could do it?"

"Son," the father replied, "I painted the vase."

This crafty painter understood a very important point: sometimes when things aren't working, you need to try something new or different to get positive results. Instead of matching the color of the walls to the vase, he did something different by painting the vase.

Likewise, when dealing with hurting relationships, you should consider trying something different. On average, most marital problems are not helped by subscribing to the "if at first you don't succeed, try, try again" rule. For example, when a problem occurs in a relationship, one spouse usually tries to fix it. If that solution works, life goes on. If it doesn't work, the fixer usually increases his efforts or does more of the same. This more-of-the-same approach maintains the problem—and more than likely intensifies it.[1]

In other words, think of solving marital problems as trying to free yourself from quicksand. The harder you try to improve the sinking relationship, the faster it dies. To free yourself from quicksand, you must try something different. Instead of kicking and screaming, you must do the opposite. To win your wife and family back, you must not become frantic and run around aimlessly in the dark. You need to relax and develop a plan. As you take very specific steps and try some new things, you free yourself from marital quicksand. Throughout the pages of this book, our goal is to expand the "try something new" concept by providing you with a detailed game plan to follow.

Can You Guarantee a Victory?

Before you run onto the field to win back your wife, we encourage you to accept that there is no guarantee of a miraculous comeback. However, you can still be victorious. If you commit yourself to the principles discussed in this book, you can greatly increase your chances of winning her back. There is no guarantee that you and your wife will reunite but, there's one thing every Christian man can hang on to by faith, regardless of your present marriage "score" or future out- come. If you will receive this difficult trial as an invitation to grow in humility and love, you will emerge the victor!

At this moment, you are right in the middle of a tremen- dous opportunity to gain unlimited yardage toward becom- ing a godly man. If you accept this painful challenge as an important wake-up call, you can gain a deeper understanding of what it means to love unconditionally. Learning to love without asking anything in return can bring you closer to Christ and make you more like Him.

In the arena of marital separation and reconciliation, you must realize that Christ needs to be your strength. Walking in step with Him and watching Him meet your deepest needs are the greatest outcomes, whatever else may happen. When you accept that Jesus is all you have, you can appreci- ate more deeply that Jesus is all you need.

Despite your pain and hopeless feelings, God will create a victory from your situation. Things could not have looked worse on that historic crucifixion afternoon. Many panicked. Many lost hope and gave up. But just three days later, God made a miraculous comeback a million times greater than the one by the Buffalo Bills—Jesus came back from the dead! Do miracles still happen? Yes, every day. A dead marriage can be resurrected! That was precisely what Jack learned when he was faced with the most painful situation of his life.

Down, But Not Out!

Jack could not have imagined the hell he was about to endure. He had no way of knowing that when he awoke for work one Wednesday morning, the top secret envelope to his private life was about to be ripped wide open.

The day before, Deanna had expected Jack home within the hour following closing time at the warehouse. As the minutes dragged on, that sick feeling in the pit of her stomach erupted all over again. Desperate to bring relief to her pangs of anxiety, she picked up the receiver to call Jack and see when she could expect him home. Would this be another one of those nights when he had to put in extra time because, in his words, he was "so swamped"?

One of the guys answered. "Yes, hi, is Jack there?" Deanna inquired.

"Deanna?" the voice asked.

"Yes, who is this?" she responded.

The voice stated, "This is Daniel. I work out in the loading area."

"I thought I recognized the voice. Listen, is Jack still there?" Deanna asked.

"Nah, he left about thirty minutes ago, I reckon," he replied.

"Okay, thanks, that's all I needed to know," she said with her heart lodged in her throat.

She hung up the phone, her thoughts swirling. Within seconds the phone rang. "Hello."

"Hello, honey, I'm still here. I thought I'd be out of here by now, but I've had to troubleshoot some major problems."

"Really?" Deanna answered suspiciously.

Jack picked up on her questioning tone and asked, "Why, what's the problem?"

"Well, Jack, I just called your office, and Daniel picked up the call to inform me that you left a half hour ago."

"Good grief," he explained. "I didn't leave to go home. I just went outside the building with a couple of the guys to straighten out this mess. Daniel probably assumed I'd taken off."

"Fine, Jack, whatever," she said with a sigh.

The doubts were piggybacking on top of every other suspicion she had had about her husband in recent months. His explanations sounded more and more like excuses, and Deanna had just about had it. The red flags were everywhere if she looked: those last-minute meetings, all those extra hours, his distancing himself more and more from her, sharing less and less, skipping church regularly, defensive moods, his short temper. *Come to think of it, he has been hounding me to take a trip to visit my sister,* she thought to herself. *Why is he so anxious for me to leave?*

Dinner and the rest of the evening were strained, but then so many of them had been lately. Deanna didn't have proof that Jack had violated their marriage vows, but all the signs were pointing there.

On Wednesday afternoon, she grabbed her car keys and purse, and she headed for the family van. She sank down into the seat and bowed her head, asking the Lord for the strength to do what she knew she had to do—confront her husband.

The moment she rounded the corner and spotted the warehouse her heart started pounding wildly. She wanted to know and didn't want to know, all at the same time. She strategically found a parking place where she could see the exit door, but no one would notice her. She waited and waited. The numbers on the dash clock seemed to stand still. After what seemed an eternity, the 4:59 finally flipped over to show 5:00. One by one, the employees filed out, making their way to their cars. But there was no sign of Jack. Should she start the van and head home?

Deanna tensely waited. The waiting came to an abrupt stop and so did her heart when, at 5:33 P.M., she spotted her husband walking out of the building with one of the female employees. Now what? What should she do? Anything? Nothing? She will never forget what she saw next. Six years of marriage and two kids later, she watched as her Christian husband got into the car, put his arm around another woman, and kissed her!

She wanted to throw up, but couldn't. She wanted to scream, but couldn't. She wanted to cry, and the floodgates opened. She couldn't drive if she wanted to, and she desperately wanted to. She finally made it home before Jack did. She had to wait again. It seemed as if all she'd done lately was to wait for him to come home.

When he walked through the front door, he spotted her in the living room, staring back at him coldly. A numbing chill swept over his body. *Does she know?* he thought.

"Hi, hon," he said softly. There was no response, only an empty stare. Moments of dead, awkward silence followed. Jack sat down across from Deanna. "What, hon? What's wrong?" he managed to ask.

Looking straight into his eyes, she announced flatly, "You've been lying to me."

Her accusation pierced him like a dagger. One look into his eyes, and Deanna knew she was on target. He had been lying. He had been unfaithful. His eyes said so. Her hurt spontaneously turned to anger.

"Here! This means nothing to me because it obviously

means nothing to you!" she screamed as she pulled off her wedding band and tossed it blindly toward him. She grabbed the closest thing within reach—his lunch box—and threw it across the room.

Jack had begun sobbing heavily as she stormed out of the living room toward their bedroom. He followed her into their bedroom, begging and pleading his case, only to hear her shout, "Get off this bed! This is my side, the pure side!" She yanked the sheets and blanket out from underneath the mattress.

It was a scene that seemed almost surreal to Jack as he stood there, motionless. *My God, what have I done?* The words played over in his mind. "I never meant for it to go this far. I never meant to hurt you," he assured her.

"You should have thought about that a long time ago . . . when I cared," she snapped. "And while you're in here, you might as well pack your clothes because I won't sleep with a adulterer!" she screamed as she walked out the door, slamming it shut.

It was beginning to sink in. Those casual encounters had led to this hell on earth. Exploding with fear and shame, Jack tried to figure out what to do next. He slumped down on his side of the bed and wondered how in the world he could fix the mess. It was amazing how one man's life, and the whole family, could shatter into a million pieces in a matter of moments.

The Rest of the Story

Jack and Deanna averted divorce. Both of them came out of their marriage trial with a deeper understanding of commitment and love for the Lord. How did they do it? How was Jack able to watch his wife go from despising him to throwing her arms around him in love? It wasn't easy, and it wasn't quick. It was accomplished one play at a time. Jack started a drive that painful day, and the momentum continues today.

Both Jack and Deanna will tell you that it took about two years to repair the damage done by his infidelity. They are now enjoying the rewards of a mutually satisfying relationship. The particular steps Jack took are woven throughout this book, and they drive home the value and importance of the relationship concepts we'll be covering.

Creating a Game Plan

As you weather your marital storm, you stand at the helm of significant choices:

- To react, or to respond.
- To meet this challenge head-on, or to take off to the high country.
- To face the struggle, or to medicate the pain through addictions.
- To find the treasure in this trial, or to bury it.
- To learn all you can, or to act as if you know it all.
- To admit the error of your ways, or to allow pride a front-row seat.

Based on more than thirty years of working with people in hurting relationships, and based on our surveys of hundreds of men and women who have experienced separation or divorce, we have developed specific steps a man can take that "score points" with his mate. On the other hand, there are behaviors that lose points with a wife. Some behaviors only weaken and threaten the whole team, while other actions put big numbers up on the marriage scoreboard. It is our desire to present a reconciliation playbook that will outline specific steps for winning your wife back. Here is a brief overview of the game plan.

Winning Your Wife Back Playbook

Step One. We want to encourage you to identify specific behaviors that are guaranteed to lose ground. We call them penalties. In the game of love you can score points in two ways. You can score by doing positive things (stringing together first downs). Or you can sustain a drive toward reconciliation by avoiding penalty flags. Penalties will keep you from gaining the valuable yardage you desire. We present nine specific penalties to avoid.

Step Two. After pointing out things that can damage the reconciliation process, we want to help you identify and understand specific patterns of behavior that can put you across the goal line consistently with your wife. Step two will help you understand why your wife may not respond to your reconciliation attempts. When you offend your wife, you usually close her spirit. Therefore, to help you gain positive yardage, we will present the secret to opening a closed spirit.

Step Three. In this step we identify the single most important principle for building healthy relationships: honoring your wife and children. Having honor within your family is like experiencing a thrilling 100-yard kickoff return!

Step Four. Related to honor is the concept of sacrificial love. In this step you will learn how important it is to prefer your wife above all other earthly things. When you become a servant to your family, contribute financially, and provide additional kinds of help, you will see firsthand how quickly the reconciliation ball moves down the field.

Step Five. Another great way to score major relational points with your wife is to initiate change in yourself. Here, you will discover four vital areas of your life that need to be balanced: mental, physical, spiritual, and social. Being in balance in these areas can make you more attractive to your wife.

Step Six. Understanding why some women are not in a position to reconcile is the next step. Your wife may have emotional baggage she is hauling around from a past relationship, and virtually nothing you do will make a significant difference in the reconciliation process. We identify three distinct reasons why some women react negatively to sincere efforts by their husbands.

Step Seven. The next important step in the reconciliation process is to understand your ultimate goal after your mate leaves. As you realize that drawing closer to the Lord is the greatest thing you can do, the joy you'll experience can make the pain worthwhile and the future look brighter.

Step Eight. Through a story about an older widow, you will understand one of the most powerful principles in life: persistence. When the process of winning your wife back seems endless, you can draw strength from God by understanding His will for your life. Can Christ restore your relationship? In this step you will find out the answer.

Step Nine. This next step will help you to identify a place where you can receive continuous support and accountability. Through this method, you can gain increased life span, higher motivation, and the perspective of others.

Step Ten. Once you're able to put some scoring drives

together and the comeback is looking very real, you need to be aware of some things if and when your wife returns. We identify several key factors in the form of a scouting report that will help you to keep your winning streak going long after the reconciliation drive ends.

Write Your Own Reconciliation Game Plan. At this point we invite you to take the valuable step of writing a personal, tailor-made game plan for winning your wife back. We will help you incorporate all of the information presented in this book into a specific contract for accountability. You can then use the reconciliation contract to gauge your progress and help others see exactly what actions you are committed to take in order to save your marriage.

Postgame Interviews. Scattered throughout this book are several stories about some couples who weathered the reconciliation process. Their stories beautifully illustrate God's will for our relationships. The postgame interviews will give you an opportunity to hear some of the most important lessons that the couples learned along the road to reconciliation. We encourage you not to miss their encouraging wisdom and insight.

Now that you have a clear picture of the reconciliation process presented throughout this book, in the words of the Buffalo Bills' coach, we invite you to "get out there and win!"

Step .... One ....

*Understand How Penalty Flags Can
Damage the Reconciliation Process*

As you enter the game of winning your wife back, you must understand certain things, or you can hurt your chances of executing the right plays. My son Greg learned how some actions can drastically damage scoring opportunities when he was playing high school football. Greg's freshman season was almost over, and he still had not done the one thing he'd dreamed of doing his whole life: scoring a touchdown!

In the last quarter of the last game something wonderful happened to Greg. His team was down by 3 points with only a few minutes left to play. Greg and his teammates were on their opponents' 15-yard line, and their chances of winning looked great. Norma and I were sitting in the stands and could barely contain ourselves. I was so pumped full of adrenaline that I felt like running down onto the field and executing the play myself.

As the ball was snapped, I grabbed Norma's arm because the quarterback was dropping back to pass. Greg was a receiver, so I knew he might get the ball. The quarterback ran around until he spotted his receiver and then released the ball. The beautiful, tight spiral seemed to hang in the air forever until it finally landed in my son's hands. "He caught it!" I screamed while almost falling off the bleachers.

"Touchdown!" was the first sound I heard after realizing that Greg had actually caught the pass. But then our excitement turned to disbelief when we realized that the referee had thrown a flag.

"What's wrong?" Norma screamed as she grabbed my arm. I had no idea.

All of the fathers quickly started second-guessing why the flag had been thrown.

"It's got to be holding."

"Did they have too many men on the field?"

"I swear I saw Billy moving before the ball was snapped!"

"Was it pass interference?"

Then suddenly someone shouted, "It was Greg! They penalized him for spiking the ball!" A big moan swept over the stands as people realized what had happened.

I couldn't believe that a referee would call something like that. As Greg ran toward the sideline with his head down, I knew that he would be heartbroken. His dream of scoring a touchdown had been dashed because of a stupid penalty. While Greg stood there facing his coach, I wondered what he must be telling him. "It's okay . . . you did your best," or "You idiot . . . your stupid antics just cost us the game!"

I didn't like thinking about the latter one. But the reality was that Greg had violated a rule, and it was costing his team the game. At least that was what we thought until someone explained that the penalty would be enforced during the extra point. The touchdown was good! And as a result of the play, Greg inherited the nickname "Spike" throughout his high school years.

Greg's actions that day serve as an important reminder as you begin the reconciliation process. Greg was penalized for spiking the ball, and you may do some things that can keep you from making positive yardage or scoring points. For example, you may quickly lose yardage when you blame your wife for the separation. Furthermore, if you become impatient during the reconciliation process and demand her return, you risk losing major yardage and may have to make up lost ground by doubling your efforts. Specifically, there are nine rules that, when violated, cause the first-down marker to move farther away and make the goal of enjoying a mutually satisfying relationship move farther still. These nine violations remind your wife how difficult it is to trust you with her feelings and may cause her to question your sincerity.

The following recommendations are not a smorgasbord of suggestions—for you to pick and choose what you like. Instead, avoiding all the penalty flags and honoring each relationship principle highlighted here can provide you with a great second-half game plan. That, in turn, will be an appealing invitation for your wife to return. But regardless of her response, becoming skilled in these relationship areas is always to your advantage.

1. Recruiting (Illegal Substitution)

During a football game, a penalty flag is dropped when there are too many players on the field. The same holds true the moment you try to recruit family and friends to your side. Siding may occur—it's human nature. However, resist the urge to campaign; allow people to respond and react as they will. Your job is to stay focused on the goal and avoid expending energy by persuading key players (family members/ friends).

George learned what can happen as a result of recruiting when he was late for a return flight from New York.

"Hurry," George said while jumping into a cab, "get me to the airport as fast as you can!" The cabbie nodded, and they took off at more than sixty miles an hour.

Just ahead a stoplight was bright red. The cab shot through the intersection without slowing down the slightest bit. "Are you blind?" shouted George. "That was a red light!"

The cabbie was unfazed. "I don't believe in red lights, sir, nor do any of my five cab-driving brothers."

After several more hair-raising hurtles through red lights, George was relieved to see a green light. Just before the intersection, however, the cabbie slammed on the brakes. "Are you insane?" screamed George. "That was a green light!"

"True, sir," replied the cabbie. "But you never know when one of my brothers may be coming through."

Attempting to recruit key players to your side can result in your learning what the New York cabbie already knew. When you recruit others, you never know when the practice will run a red light and come back to hurt you. Recruiting draws a penalty flag because of its boomerang effect—it potentially can come hurling back. As this happens, it becomes very difficult to accomplish your goal of reconciliation because your wife is almost always driven farther away.

In every situation there is a way to respond that is best. But the reverse is also true. For example, the urge to share your side with your kids can be difficult to resist. You may feel that they are getting only part of the whole picture or a one-sided view. If you sincerely believe that lies or partial truths are being communicated, pray that truth will be revealed, then trust the Lord. The negative ripple effect of taking sides, or recruiting, is far-reaching. Therefore, hold on to the truth of Romans 8:31 (NKJV): "If God is for us, who can be against us?"

2. Blaming (Intentional Grounding)

Closely tied to recruiting is the penalty flag of blame. Someone wisely observed, "A man can make many mistakes, but he isn't a failure until he starts blaming someone else."[1]

Blaming your wife for the marital problems can leave others with a distorted image of the situation. John was a blamer. He didn't like his job, he struggled through all of his relationships, and he couldn't get ahead financially. He was convinced that if he could somehow escape the real world and its troubles, he would be happy. That thought process led John to enter a monastery.

The monastery had an excellent reputation. The monks there really knew how to forsake the world's allure, which appealed to John, so he gladly signed on. At his first meeting with the monsignor, John learned about the code of discipline. "My son," the monsignor began, "at this monastery we abide by a strict code of silence. Consequently, you will be allowed to speak only once every five years, and when you do speak, you will be limited to two words."

John reluctantly agreed and went about his life at the monastery for five years. Year after year he searched for the real meaning of life in the halls of silence. When the first five years were up, the monsignor called John to his office for the opportunity to speak.

"All right, my son, you may speak your two words."

Without a moment's hesitation, John opened his mouth and uttered his feelings. "Food bad!"

John left the monsignor's office and went about his duties faithfully for another five years. At his ten-year anniversary at the monastery, he was called in to the monsignor's office for the uttering of the words. Once again, John wasted no time and quickly blurted out, "Bed hard!"

John quietly left the office to work another five years in silence. After fifteen years in the monastery, John took the opportunity to express how he felt. The whole experience had been too much for him, so he merely said, "I quit!"

The monsignor fired back, "Well, I'm not surprised. All you've done since you've been here is complain!"

John never seemed able to see the good of monastery life. Instead, he chose to blame his problems on trivial things. Likewise, when you blame your wife for your current situation, you rob yourself of taking advantage of the reconciliation game plan. Football players know that one of the best ways to beat the opposing team is to defeat them mentally, so they will start fighting among themselves. The same is true in your relationship. Blaming your wife makes winning almost impossible because arguments and fighting usually result. As you try to run your reconciliation plays, blaming has the same tragic effect as tackling one of your own players.

We encourage you to resist making "you" statements such as, "You're the one who needs to change," "You should have warned me that our marriage was in trouble," "You're not the same woman I married," and "You weren't submissive enough," as reasons for *your* behavior. These "you" statements are devastating, and they seldom improve your situation. Therefore, to win your wife back, avoid using these types of blaming statements. The most important reason is found in Proverbs 15:1 (NKJV): "A soft answer turns away wrath, but a harsh word stirs up anger."

Using a statement such as, "You were just too sensitive," stirs up more anger in your wife. As this happens, the blaming backfires and exposes your resistance to improve or change. Just as the Buffalo Bills felt hopeless going into half time down by 25 points, your wife may lose hope when faced with blaming. Try to keep your focus on improving your character and loving your wife by meeting her needs. When you experience the urge to blame your wife, remember King Solomon's wise words: "A man of knowledge uses words with restraint, and a man of understanding is even-tempered" (Prov. 17:27 NIV).

3. Having a Critical Spirit (Unsportsmanlike Conduct)

Pointing out every black spot on your wife's white uniform deserves an unsportsmanlike penalty every time. Lecturing your wife seldom produces the results you desire. Demeaning and dishonoring speech usually breeds only contempt. She'll not only refuse to play on your team, but she'll refuse to suit up, keeping her nowhere near the playing field.

A young man saw firsthand how harmful critical words can be as he boarded a plane. He sat down next to an elegant woman wearing the largest, most stunning diamond ring he had ever seen. He asked her about it.

"This is the famous White diamond," she said. "It is beautiful, but a dreadful curse goes with it."

"What's the curse?" the young man asked.

"Mr. White!"

As the wife criticized her husband, imagine what the young man must have thought of Mr. White. *Poor guy! How did such a rich man get to be so stupid!* or *What in the world did he do to deserve that?*

When you heap criticism on your wife—her looks, her decisions, her thoughts, her likes or dislikes, her plans, her handling of the family, or her managing of things—you do damage that may lead her to never see you again. No one enjoys playing for a coach who continually rants and raves, barks out orders, throws headsets, and rides everyone's back (especially if he has made wrong decisions in the past).

4. Being Impatient (Encroachment)

One of the strangest football bloopers I ever saw took place during the final minutes of a hometown game years ago. Down by 5 points, the home team needed to stop their opponents from getting a first down. Unless they were stopped, the other team would kick a field goal and put the game out of reach. It was third down and 9 yards to go, so the opposition set up in a passing formation, meaning they had five receivers and no running backs.

Seconds before the ball was snapped, a linebacker from the home team tried to guess the snap count, so he could hurdle the center and sack the quarterback. The linebacker got about 10 yards back and came flying toward the line. Unfortunately for him, the quarterback saw what he was doing and stepped aside. However, the center didn't realize what was happening. When the quarterback moved, the ball was snapped, and it went rolling back unguarded. The amazing part was, the linebacker had flown about 5 yards past the line of scrimmage, and the ball bounced right to him. The home crowd went wild as he raced 60 yards for an apparent touchdown. When the celebration died down, everyone realized that the linebacker had been penalized for encroachment. No touchdown! The worst part was that with the penalty yardage, the opposing team easily picked up the first down and went on to win the game.

In the reconciliation process, an encroachment penalty flag comes flying out when you become impatient. If you become too anxious like that linebacker, you might miss a golden opportunity to win back your wife's trust. As you respect your wife by giving her the gift of space, you can turn the momentum back toward your side. Do not fear that the reconciliation process will be slowed down unless you are in contact. God can bridge any gap.

Regard this separation period as part of your training program. To build up strength and get his body into shape, a player must spend many hours in the weight room. Consider this separation as exactly that—you're spending time in the "wait" room. You can use this time to build your relational muscles by developing friendships with people who can encourage your spiritual growth and hold you accountable. Use this time to humbly wait on God's will for your life by living out Matthew 22:37–40 (NIV): "'Love the Lord your God with all your heart and with all your soul and with all your mind.' This is the first and greatest commandment. And the second is like it: 'Love your neighbor as yourself.' All the Law and the Prophets hang on these two commandments."

5. Setting a Time Frame (Illegal Snap)

One penalty flag that will be thrown sky-high results from imposing a time frame on your wife for reconciliation. In other words, you try to control the game clock. By trying to control her response to you, we mean using comments like these: "It's been long enough . . . You should be able to trust me by now . . . How long are you going to punish me?"

A naval captain learned the dangers of trying to control others when in the pitch-black night, he realized that his ship was on a collision course with another ship. With the collision alarm blaring, he sent a message to the approaching vessel: "Change your course ten degrees east."

As all eyes were focused in the direction of the approaching object, suddenly, a signal in return read, "Change yours, ten degrees west."

"*What?*" the captain furiously shouted. "Who does this guy think I am?" Angry, the captain sent: "I'm a navy captain! Change your course, sir!"

"I'm a seaman, second class," came the reply. "Change your course, sir."

The captain was enraged. "I'm a battleship! I'm not changing course!"

There was one last reply: "I'm a lighthouse. Your call."

Like the navy captain's attempts to manipulate the lighthouse, your attempts to control the situation could cause your wife to become an immovable rock and resent you more deeply. As a result, she may interpret your control as a lack of understanding and may extend the time that she spends apart from you.

Another way to receive a controlling penalty is to spiritualize your efforts to win her back. For example, saying, "The Bible says that a godly woman submits to her husband," or "I know God wants us back together now," can only increase the distance between you.

You must understand that your wife processes decisions differently. Every person's built-in timer is different, and one cannot impose the right time on another. For example, a sponge will make it to the bottom of a pool more slowly than a rock. Some women are like sponges and soak up things more slowly. Other women are like rocks and hit bottom faster. Wait on her until she is ready to reenter the game.

"What Kind of Time Frame Is Involved?"

If you are asking yourself, How much time does she need before I can ask her to come back? remember a very important principle: the greater the hurt, the longer the healing time.

Anyone who follows football knows that a severe injury sidelines a player longer than a muscle spasm or cramp does. A broken bone immediately puts a player on the injured reserve list. It's no different for a marital injury. Emotional pain and scars require lots of *time* to heal. If you rush the process, she might feel like a player sent back into the game with a broken leg or, worse, while still on a stretcher.

If your wife needs more time, she is really saying that the hurt is deeper than you realized. She is probably attempting to communicate that you don't fully understand the depth of her pain or the disappointment and she doesn't trust the relationship enough to commit herself again. If she opens herself up to you one more time—and your changes prove temporary, manipulative, or insincere—her hopes can be crushed forever. Her heart may not be able to take one more major disappointment from you. It may be all she can do to muster the courage to put herself in such a vulnerable position again.

Trust is a major issue for a wife considering reconciliation. If you are to win your wife back, the relationship needs security to grow and thrive. In all our research, a marriage supported by the bedrock of security can best stand up to the inevitable storms of life. Conversely, insecurity can do major damage, causing the entire structure of marriage to shake and crumble. What do we mean by security?

Security—or trust—is the assurance that someone is committed to love and value you for a lifetime. It's the constant awareness that whatever difficulties both of you face, you'll work to solve the problems together. Security means that you're fully committed to the truth, and you make a decision to be open to correction.[2] You build security into your relationship each time you speak the truth, go out of your way to encourage, listen without lecturing, or give a gentle hug. You tear down the trust level in a home with the opposite *behavior*—lying (even white lies), not keeping a check on tone of voice or volume control, or being harsh instead of soft.

When it comes to building a bridge of intimacy in your marriage, is your pillar of security a solid one? Without pressure or nonverbal threats, if you asked your spouse how secure she feels in your relationship, how would she answer?

On a scale of 1 to 10, how secure do you feel in your relationship? Is your security level where it needs to be? Does your spouse share your perspective?

1   2   3   4   5   6   7   8   9   10
Little Security   Great Security

Whatever the circumstances surrounding your separation or divorce, trust has certainly been broken. Trust must be restored before the relationship can be reconstructed. Although it may take many years for the trust to be completely renewed, you can do certain things to aid this process. You can help your wife to recover from her injuries and you can rebuild trust by giving her plenty of time and space. Many more wives desire to reconcile than actually do; your wife may be one of them. If she is, then she is probably feeling drawn to reconcile but must resist because she cannot bring herself to take that difficult leap of faith—just yet. Remember, "be anxious for nothing, but in everything by prayer and supplication, with thanksgiving, let your requests be made known to God" (Phil. 4:6 NKJV).

6. Displaying Affection in Physical Ways (Holding)

Though you may be highly motivated and sincere in wanting to express your love, affection, and appreciation for your wife, resist the urge to do so, or you may get a 10-yard penalty for holding. You must be extremely cautious when you initiate physical displays of affection. That doesn't mean you must turn into a cold fish. It means you purposely become more sensitive to what she wants and when she wants it. If your wife is like most women, the last thing she wants right now is anything intimate or sexual.

Although the sexual needs of a man and a woman are certainly very important, the differences between them are striking. In some ways, a man is like a microwave. He is ready for the sexual union in a matter of seconds. But the average woman is more like a Crock-Pot. It takes her much longer—in some cases hours or even days of being treated like a valuable person—to emotionally desire to share physical intimacy with her husband. Many men don't realize it, but more than 80 percent of a woman's need for meaningful touch is non-sexual.[3]

Sex doesn't begin in the bedroom. It begins in the everyday acts of truthfulness, consistency, kindness, touching, and talking that build a growing desire in a woman. If she initiates any expressions, respond appropriately, but do not take the ball and run with it. You can tell her that you feel affectionate toward her, and that you would like to demonstrate it, but you recognize her hurt is so great that any physical display may be inappropriate and uncomfortable for her. Even if your wife left you because you were not affectionate, do not dive in now by demonstrating it. You can tell her that you've gotten the message, and that you want to treat her as she deserves to be treated, but you will wait for the day when she tells you that she is comfortable with it again—however long that takes.

7. Overkilling (Piling On)

Along the same line as being too aggressive with displays of affection, you can be penalized if you overkill with flowers, cards, and gifts. You may feel like the husband who wanted to improve his marriage, so he joined a weekly accountability group. One day, the man became convicted for not having expressed his appreciation to his wife more often. He left work early and bought his wife some flowers, candy, and a card. With great pride he presented the gifts and exclaimed, "Hi, honey! I love you so much!"

Immediately, his wife started crying. "Everything's gone wrong today," she explained, sobbing. "The baby's grouchy, the dishwasher won't work, and now you come home drunk!"

Flowery actions, done now, may smell like a bribe to your wife. She might wonder, *Why now?* but she already knows the answer. You're on a mission to get her back—out to conquer her. If reconciliation takes place, then flowers, cards, and gifts will be tangible and welcomed expressions of love. Women generally see gifts as symbolic expressions, saying something about the giver and the recipient. Your wife will know if your gifts stem from motives of love or selfish manipulation. If she senses a possible bribe, there isn't a florist shop big enough to persuade her otherwise. Cards, gifts, and flowers need to reflect where you are in a relationship, not where you hope to be.

What constitutes overkill is different for each person, but a good general rule of thumb is this: if your gifts are too frequent and too extravagant, you've probably gone overboard or done too much. Less is best. If you feel you must have contact, write her, and share what you are learning during this valuable timeout.

8. Underestimating Hurt (Unnecessary Roughness)

A guaranteed 15-yard unnecessary roughness penalty happens when you discount or minimize the hurt your wife is experiencing or how much pain you may have caused. You may feel that the issues dividing you were not bad enough to warrant a separation or divorce. Or perhaps you feel that she was equally responsible for the marriage problems. Although there can be some truth in these feelings, your wife may not be feeling that way. Understanding that men and women feel and perceive things differently is a play that will guarantee positive yardage in the game to win back your wife.

Unfortunately, a young lawyer did not understand the effects of underestimating others' pain. A junior partner in a law firm called in his staff for a meeting. "I have good news and bad news," he said, smiling. "Which do you want first?" The staff moaned and decided to hear the bad news first. "Okay," said the junior partner. "Half of you won't be here tomorrow because we are downsizing. Furthermore, those of you who don't get fired may stay at a considerable reduction in salary."

The staff sat in horrified shock. Finally, someone asked in a trembling voice, "What's the good news?"

The boss lit up with excitement. "I've been made a full partner!"

Focusing on yourself during this time may cause additional problems between you and your wife. Imagine how those employees felt when, after being told they might get fired, their boss informed them of *his* success. Many of the employees probably thought, *Great, at least I don't have to work for this jerk any longer.* When you focus on your pain or issues while underestimating your wife's hurt, she may no longer want to "work" with you, either.

Another way to understand this principle is to picture yourself as a grazing water buffalo. If someone placed a tiny pebble on your back, your movement would not be slowed, and you probably wouldn't even know it was there. Because women tend to be more sensitive than men, picture your wife as a delicate monarch butterfly. What would happen if you placed that same small pebble on one of her wings? She would instantly get smashed into the ground! Most women feel everything more intensely than men do. Each time you underestimate her pain, you are stacking pebbles on your wife's wings. Likewise, when you try to counter her hurt by sharing how much pain you're in, you've just plopped a boulder on her.

As you attempt to win back your wife, you score points by focusing on your wife's pain. Realize that she has probably been hurting a long time. You can keep the situation from escalating by listening to her perceived pain instead of arguing or being defensive. King Solomon understood this when he encouraged believers by writing, "A man of understanding holds his tongue" (Prov. 11:12 NIV). If you desire to become a man of understanding, then we encourage you to ask your wife to list the ways you hurt her and disappointed her, how you may have neglected or abused her, and how she felt unappreciated and unloved. This is a valuable exercise because if she responds, it will provide you with a checklist from which to work and score points.

9. *Disregarding Boundaries (Offsides)*

In football, there are consequences when players disregard or violate the boundary lines. For example, when a player lines up in the neutral zone or a quarterback steps beyond the line of scrimmage to deliver a pass, valuable yardage is lost. Boundaries define the playing field and rules of the game, and no contest can be played without them.

The same holds true in marital relationships. In life, boundaries define who we are. In other words, each person has individual needs, wants, aspirations, dreams, interests, ideas, beliefs, habits, and mannerisms.

No lasting relationship is possible without boundaries. If you continually walk on, ignore, criticize, or minimize your wife's boundaries, she may grow to resent you and will probably question your love for her.

I seriously disregarded Norma's boundaries when we had been married about ten years. At the time, I was working for a Christian ministry. One day my boss and I were discussing some new marriage material on what it means for a wife to have a "quiet spirit." My boss felt a "quiet spirit" meant that wives submitted to their husbands without question or discussion. I mentioned to my boss that maybe I should share these ideas with my wife, Norma. He challenged me to encourage Norma to give up her most prized possession until she developed a quiet spirit. Although the idea seemed strange, I wanted to please my boss. I went home that day unaware of the damage I was about to heap upon my wife.

After the kids were in bed, I approached Norma about how her spirit wasn't as quiet and submissive as it could be. "Norma," I said cautiously, "what is your most prized possession?" Looking back on the situation after more than twenty years, I wish she had said it was me! But I wasn't going to be that fortunate.

"The kids, I suppose," Norma answered suspiciously. Knowing that she would rather give me up than our children, I quickly shot back, "Besides the children, what is your favorite possession?" Norma thought about it for some time—almost as if she knew where I was leading her with my question. Finally, she blurted out, "I guess it would be my wedding ring."

Over the next few minutes I explained that she should give this prized possession to the Lord until she had a quiet spirit. Norma handed over the ring without so much as a whisper. However, she didn't really need to say anything because her eyes revealed the tremendous hurt she felt. We didn't speak for the next several hours. It was difficult to sleep that night because something wasn't right about what I had done. Norma was hurting so badly on the inside that I hadn't realized how tightly I had closed her spirit.

The next day, the events of the past night kept gnawing at me. I left work early and rushed home. When I saw Norma, I realized that I had disregarded her boundaries. I instantly asked her to forgive me and promised that someday I would buy her a beautiful new ring for dishonoring her that day.

One of the happiest days of my life was seeing Norma's eyes light up when I got down on bended knee and presented her with a new ring several years later. If someone asked about her most prized possession, besides her faith and her family, she would proudly say, "It's my wedding ring!"

As I did to Norma, when you impose your boundaries or do not respect your mate's uniqueness, you dishonor her. She will probably throw a penalty flag every time, believing you are trying to control her. When you line up in her neutral zone and violate her boundaries, it's called invalidation.

According to marital experts Dr. Scott Stanley and Dr. Howard Markman, one of the main reasons for divorce is that one spouse doesn't allow the other spouse to be a unique person—complete with needs and wants. Drs. Stanley and Markman say that invalidation is "a pattern in which one partner subtly or directly puts down the thoughts, feelings, or character of the other."[4] That is, you are not allowing your wife to be an individual.

Your mate is your equal, your adult partner, and needs to be treated as such. You are at risk for violating her boundaries each time you attempt to control her or the reconciliation process. Talking to her as a parent to a child, flaring up in a jealous rage, or restricting her freedoms invalidates or violates her boundaries. Furthermore, whenever you pout, sulk, withdraw, or answer her with indifference, you run the risk of being penalized. If you fall behind in the score or receive a 5-yard penalty, remember that love is freeing, not controlling. When your wife feels her uniqueness is being honored and respected, the original flame can be rekindled.

In the next step, we are going to discuss an unbelievably powerful emotion that all of us have, yet few of us master. It has the potential to make our lives more meaningful and our relationships more fulfilling—or it can literally destroy the very things that are most precious to us. Understanding it is absolutely essential if we want to honor God and others. Let's discover the secrets to mastering what may be the most powerful of all human emotions.

Cautionary Warning for a Man Who Has Battered His Wife

We strongly suggest to a man whose wife has left because of aggression to back off for a period of time. Furthermore, he needs to radically pursue a changed life through walking with God and seeking appropriate counseling, but he should not pursue the wife who does not currently want (or may never want) to be pursued. Some of these marriages can be healed (especially ones where there have been less severe abuse and control, along with real repentance and change). But in no way is our game plan designed to encourage a batterer to infringe on the boundaries of his wife when she is probably doing all she can to get distance and be safe.

Step ....
Two ....

Open a Closed Spirit

Beware: Dangerous Cliff Ahead!

Many years ago there was a preacher who decided to sell his mountain trail horse. A prospective buyer was impressed with the animal's skill and obedience. Before they agreed on a price, the preacher said, "I must warn you—he responds only to spiritual commands. To get the horse moving, you say, 'Praise the Lord,' and stop is 'Hallelujah.'"

"I've been around horses all my life," said the buyer, "and I've never heard of anything like this." Mounting the horse, he said skeptically, "Praise the Lord." The horse began to trot. He repeated, "Praise the Lord," and the horse broke into a gallop. Suddenly, the buyer realized that a cliff was dead ahead. Frantically, he yelled, "Hallelujah," and they came to a stop a foot from the edge. Wiping the sweat from his brow, the buyer said, "Praise the Lord!"

Now is not the time to shout, "Praise the Lord!" Like the man riding his new horse, you may think you've learned how to ride the reconciliation horse, but one mistake can send you flying over the cliff. You may feel more confident now that you believe you can avoid the nine penalty flags, but your reconciliation game is not won without some offensive plays as well.

Identifying First-Down Markers

To move toward making a first down in your marital relationship, consider this equation: "If you sow bountifully, you will reap bountifully." That is, positive behaviors reap positive rewards. Women naturally respond to things that positively enhance relationships. In this book we will focus on several positive relational "plays" that can help you move toward enjoying a mutually satisfying relationship with your wife.

As you receive the kickoff, the opening drive begins with thanking the Lord. Thank Him for giving you an opportunity to grow because that's what this time apart really is: "In everything give thanks; for this is the will of God in Christ Jesus for you" (1 Thess. 5:18 NKJV). It couldn't be clearer. Saying "thank you" to Jesus (and not shaking your fist skyward) is God's desire for your life. Thank the Lord for being a God of second and third and fourth chances. Thank Him for not giving up on you and for standing ready to help you grow by this challenge.

Next, thank your wife. Thank her for getting your attention through such a courageous act. Thank her for not tolerating your unloving behavior any longer and for sending you on a course of learning how to become a better husband and father. As you express thanks to your wife, you take a major step in winning her back. Essentially what you are doing is part of one of the most powerful techniques we've found to release your wife from the anger that binds her. This next method that we'll be sharing is the single most significant factor in establishing and maintaining harmony within relationships.

A Closed Spirit

In my life and counseling ministry, the single most significant factor in dealing with unresolved anger is illustrated by something that happened to my granddaughter when she was about a year old. One day Taylor was playing with her father, Greg, in the backyard when she discovered a bunch of sow bugs. She was fascinated whenever she touched the bugs, and they rolled up into little balls. Since Taylor loves anything round, she kept flicking the bugs and squealing "Ball! Ball!"

After being distracted for a few moments, Greg turned toward Taylor and was horrified to see several sow bugs rolling around in her mouth. With her mouth full, Taylor was pointing to the remaining bugs on the ground and was shrieking, "Ball! Ball!"

Greg quickly did the "finger sweep" and rushed her inside. Since dads usually get blamed for these things, Greg knew that he was in big trouble when they reached Taylor's mother. Unfortunately, the only thing he could think to say was, "At least she got plenty of protein!"

This story has more to do with your situation than you realize. The sow bug has three distinct parts: a protective shell, body, and organs. God created every person with three interrelated parts as well: body, soul, and spirit. The body is the physical makeup. The soul includes the mind, will, and emotions. The spirit is the innermost being, like the conscience; we have fellowship with one another at this level.

In healthy families, each person relates to the others on all three levels. Everyone's body language communicates openness; family members are free to speak, to think, and to feel, all of which communicate to each person's spirit. And with many positive exchanges, relationships grow deeper in the three areas. However, a person can also be offended, causing his spirit to close.

The sow bugs illustrate what happens when your wife is offended. Before Taylor started playing with them, the bugs were completely open and vulnerable. But when she started flicking them, they closed up into tight balls. In a similar way, when your wife is offended, her spirit, soul, and body close.

What Happens When Your Wife's Spirit Closes?

Although there are probably hundreds of ways to offend your wife and close her spirit, we consistently see several that top the list. You can close your wife's spirit by

- speaking harsh words.
- telling her that her opinions don't matter.
- being unwilling to admit when you are wrong.
- taking her for granted.
- making jokes or sarcastic comments at her expense.
- not trusting her.
- forcing her to do something that she's uncomfortable with.

- being rude to her in front of others.
- dismissing her needs as unimportant.[1]

Your wife could probably make up her own list of the things you've done that closed her spirit.

At our office in Branson, Missouri, we consistently get calls from men all around the world who are desperate because their wives just walked out the door. The most devastating part is that many of these men fail to realize that little by little, their actions closed their wives' spirits. Because this happens internally, many men don't realize that they've offended their wives. And one day the husband comes home to find his wife's spirit rolled up in a tight ball, like the sow bug. You may not always be aware of what you do to deposit anger into the life of your loved one. However, when it comes to relationships, a preventive rule of thumb is this: whatever dishonors another person usually closes her spirit!

If you have been wondering why your wife left or perhaps why she resists your efforts at reconciliation, the answer is usually found in a closed spirit. The sad reality is, the more a man steps on the spirit of his wife, the more resistant she becomes to him. It's fairly easy to identify a closed spirit once you know what to look for. The most common signs of a closed spirit are listed here:

- She often has an argumentative attitude.
- Her facial expressions reflect anger or avoidance.
- She is very resistant to discussing or agreeing on almost anything.
- Her hand is often cold and unresponsive when you touch it.

- You sense she is avoiding you.
- She often turns her back away from you.
- She does not respect your advice.
- She can become very critical of you.
- She has no or few romantic or warm feelings toward you.
- She walks out the door or files for legal separation or divorce![2]

Our purpose in writing about a closed spirit is not to make you—who may find yourself with a closed sow bug instead of an open wife—feel guilty. It is to provide hope. I have done many things to close the spirit of my wife and the key to reconciliation is to learn how to reopen her spirit.

In the last chapter I told the story of taking Norma's wedding ring away until she developed a submissive spirit. Well, that was probably one of my worst cases of causing Norma's spirit to close. When I came home from work that day, I had to do several specific things to dissolve Norma's anger and hurt, thus allowing her spirit to reopen.

Let me state clearly that you can't mechanically go down the list and expect to erase every hurt or drain away all the anger in a relationship. With Norma, it took me only a half hour to reopen her spirit and reestablish harmony. On the other hand, when a wife takes the difficult step to leave her husband, her spirit is usually closed very tightly. Therefore, it may take months or even years before she can be completely reopened and total harmony can be restored.

However, the time involved is not the focal point. You must make the decision and commitment to do whatever is necessary to release your wife's anger. For years now, I have practiced the following four attitudes to make sure that anger is drained out of our home on a daily basis.

Four Attitudes That Can Help to Open a Closed Spirit

1. Become Soft and Tender with Your Wife

What I mean by tenderness is illustrated by something that happened to an older couple who had been married fifty years. The wife was trying to help her husband remember how to be soft. "Things have really changed over the years," she said. "You used to sit close to me."

"Well, I can correct that," he said, moving next to her on the couch.

"Remember how much you loved to snuggle?"

"How's that?" he asked his wife while giving her a gentle hug.

"But of all the things you did that drove me totally wild," she explained, "the best was nibbling on my earlobe!"

Suddenly, the man jumped to his feet and ran from the room. "Where are you going?" his wife shouted.

"I'll be right back," he exclaimed. "I've got to get my teeth!"

Proverbs 15:1 (NKJV) says, "A soft answer turns away wrath." My whole problem with Norma started when I became harsh and unreasonable and violated her boundaries. As it happened with the older couple, things started to turn around when I used a softer tone of speech. My attitude, nonverbals, signals, and voice said I cared about her. It is amazing how powerful becoming soft and tender can be. Sometimes softness is all it takes to reopen a closed spirit.

When a man shows his tender side, it's as successful as

splitting the uprights on a field goal. But before you think I am asking you to become Mr. Sensitive, understand that softness does not mean you clock out your rational and logical side at work, and begin watching tearjerker movies at home.

On the contrary, I am talking about controlled strength. As I attempted to reopen Norma's closed spirit, I needed to carefully understand what King Solomon meant when he wrote, "A fool gives full vent to his anger, but a wise man keeps himself under control" (Prov. 29:11 NIV).

Instead of attacking Norma or being defensive, I needed to be strong by controlling my words and behaviors. When a husband has this controlled strength, he is free to give his wife the tenderness that is required to reopen her spirit. In other words, he needs to provide compassion, kindness, understanding, and nonsexual affection. All of these softer tendencies come more easily when you "feel" your wife's pain. When you understand exactly what she felt when you offended her—and you feel remorse for your actions—you develop tenderness.

Many men experience difficulty being soft and tender because of a common misconception. For generations we have been told that when a man drops his guard and shows his vulnerability (his fears, anxieties, concerns, or inadequacies), his wife will panic and feel that she can't depend on him. A man reasons, "If I show her any weakness whatsoever, either I'll not be the strong man she needs, or she'll take advantage of me." Unfortunately, along with this misconception is the curse of trying to appear that he is completely adequate every waking hour, in every situation.

Ironically, a woman's true desire is the opposite of this misconception. When a man shares his feelings with his wife, she feels closer to him than ever before (even if he admits that he doesn't know what to do in a given situation, that he is anxious about something pending, or that he is so discouraged he feels he can't go on). At these times, a wife feels at one with her husband—and the closest to him. Women interpret this true confession as strength, not weakness. That was what King Solomon was speaking about in Proverbs 29:11.

In his wife's eyes, a husband is never more manly than when he is open and honest about his innermost feelings. For example, remember the heartful broadcast several years ago when Barbara Walters interviewed General Norman Schwarzkopf? He is a national hero, a role model, and a man's man if there ever was one. No one doubts his tough side. But he is especially captivating because his hard side is balanced by softness. On camera, the beloved general told us about his teddy bear collection and was not apologetic about shedding tears. Did he appear weak on national TV? Not on your life—thousands of women fought back instant crushes.

The good news is that you can change. Instead of closing your wife's spirit by lecturing her, or by being harsh, impatient, or selfish, you can rack up valuable rushing yardage as game-breakers Walter Payton and Emmitt Smith do every time you show her tenderness. You may be feeling tender toward your wife right now, but she gives every indication that she couldn't care less. Stay with it: "Let us not become weary in doing good, for at the proper time we will reap a harvest if we do not give up" (Gal. 6:9 NIV).

Don't forget: your wife didn't lose her love for you overnight, and you can't rekindle it in a single day.

2. Understand, as Much as Possible, What Your Wife Has Gone Through

I would have been hurt and angry if Norma had demanded that I give up my most prized possession simply because her boss felt it was the right thing to do. Through my words, I showed Norma that I understood how she might have felt. I repeated how awful it must have been, trying not to react defensively to what she was saying. During the time of understanding and listening, a good rule of thumb is to listen to what is said; do not react to the words used.

One of the all-time relationship plays is in this area of listening. When a man truly listens to a woman, he scores major points. Listening communicates that you feel she has something valuable to say; consequently, she feels valuable. Listening shows that you respect her as a teammate. Make your desire to hear your wife be greater than trying to be heard. Listen to understand rather than to respond. Listen to her with your heart—hear her pain and feel her needs.

When you are really listening, you don't need to tell anybody—it's evident. You can bet your wife knows whether you're truly listening or faking it. You show you're listening by body language, nonverbal responses using facial expressions and eye contact, and questions. Furthermore, you pick up cues or signals to give evidence of paying attention. Here are characteristics of a good listener:

- He is attentive; he does not look around or do something else at the same time.
- He does not rush the speaker.
- He is focused on the person speaking.

- He does not interrupt.
- He makes good eye contact.
- He does not grunt responses.

When you're really listening to your wife, you focus your attention squarely on her. She will feel that she is the most important person in the world. Listening does not require attempts at problem solving. She merely wants to know that you understand her point of view. She wants to sense from you that it's okay to be upset or emotional.

Good listening takes time. That's why so few people practice it, much less master it. Know this: if your wife does not feel that she is being heard, she'll not likely grant you greater contact. To the degree she feels listened to, it's to that degree she will grant you opportunities for communication. Who wants to talk to someone who doesn't listen? For that matter, who wants to live with someone who doesn't listen? Therefore, as you attempt to understand how your wife feels or what she has been through, we encourage you to use a powerful communication method that instantly allows you to hear and completely understand your wife.

Using drive-through listening for greater understanding. Picture yourself at a local fast-food drive-through window. You've stopped at the speaker box to place your order. You look over the menu and select several food items that will meet your needs. "May I take your order?" says a voice.

"Yes," you say confidently. "I'll have a cheeseburger, fries, and a large Coke."

There's a short moment of silence, and then the voice repeats, "You want a burger, fries, and a large diet?"

"Close," you shout in the direction of the speaker box, "but I want a *cheeseburger*, fries, and a large *Coke*."

"Sorry, sir," the box says with remorse. "You want a cheeseburger, fries, and a large Coke. Will that be all?"

"That'll do it," you insist.

"That will be $3.05. Please pull up to the second window and have a nice day."

The purpose of this verbal exchange is twofold. First, you help the employee clearly and accurately understand your order. You don't pay until you're satisfied that you've been understood and receive the items you ordered. Second, the people at restaurants are satisfied when they hear you correctly and get paid. This is a good example of the meaningful communication that should take place in marriage.

If there is an issue to discuss in your marriage, one of you becomes the person in the car, and the other becomes the restaurant employee. The customer first explains what he is feeling or needing. For example, "I feel dishonored when I come home and you instantly want me to fix something." Be sure to use "I feel" statements as opposed to "you" statements ("you make me feel . . ." is a yellow flag).

Next, the employee repeats what she heard you say: "Did I hear you say that you do not like doing work around the house?" Once she repeats what she thought you said, then you have an opportunity to edit or amend her interpretation.

"Close," you explain. "It's not that I don't like to work around the house. Instead, I'm saying that I feel dishonored when I come home from a long day and you immediately give me little jobs to do. I would rather spend some time with the kids unwinding first. Then after dinner I would be happy to fix whatever you need." Your wife repeats your statement until you feel she understands your feelings and needs.

When you have finished sharing and she understands what you were trying to communicate, she gets to talk. You trade places. Your wife becomes the customer, and you get to be the employee. She places her order by explaining how she feels or what she needs. Your job is to repeat what you hear her communicating.

"Honey," your wife begins to explain, "I feel frustrated. I ask you when you first get home because you get so busy with something else that you won't do what I need."

"So you're saying that you feel upset because unless you ask me right away, I'll ignore your requests," you repeat.

"Yes," she says excitedly. "That's exactly right. I feel if I don't ask right away, then you'll ignore me."

Although this is just an example, can you see how excited a woman can get when she feels understood? It's a great way to melt away the anger and frustration. This wife may have been very upset with her husband because he constantly ignored her requests. She probably felt that she was last on his list of priorities. But because he used the drive-through talking method, she felt that he really understood her feelings and needs.

You should use short sentences with each other so that you can repeat precisely what was said. Once each person understands the other completely, you can begin the process of determining a solution. Solutions tend to come when each understands the other's feelings and needs.

Consider this time of separation as an opportunity for you to become a better listener and communicator. You don't learn how to be a good listener by reading all about it.

Instead, you learn how to listen by actively listening, using drive-through talking. The Scriptures identify this practice as a worthy effort, promising wisdom and success! "He who cherishes understanding prospers . . . Listen to advice and accept instruction, and in the end you will be wise" (Prov. 19:8, 20 NIV).[3]

This method is such a powerful communication tool that it works well with children, adolescents, coworkers, and friends. We encourage you to become an expert in this area because the rewards of effective communication can be limitless.

3. Acknowledge That Your Wife Is Hurting, Then Admit Your Mistake and Seek Forgiveness

Perhaps your wife feels like one of the monkeys at a local zoo. "That's unbelievable, having a lion and a monkey in the same cage," said the visitor to a small zoo. "How do they get along?"

"Pretty good usually," replied the zookeeper. "Occasionally they have a disagreement, and we have to get a new monkey."

Your wife may feel that each time the two of you get into a disagreement, you come down on her like a strong lion. Perhaps she is wounded or feels that her spirit has been "killed," like one of those monkeys. She may feel that you simply replaced her instead of tending to her wounds by admitting your wrongdoing. As a husband, you may find it very hard to say, "I was wrong," but as I discovered with Norma, it usually works wonders. Admitting you are wrong (when you clearly are) is like tending to your wife's wounds. It's like drilling a hole in your loved one's "anger bucket" and allowing the unhealthy emotion to drain away. Once she hears you admit it, the anger has a way of escaping from her life.

Sometimes you may be right, but your attitude may not be. Or maybe the way you've done something is offensive. If your attitude is harsh and angry even when telling about legitimate problems, you can still be in the wrong: "Man's anger [or that of a woman] does not bring about the righteous life that God desires" (James 1:20 NIV). Stopping short of admitting you're wrong can leave a dangerous gap between you and your wife, which may not mend quickly—or at all.

Seeking forgiveness. After you admit your mistakes, the reconciliation ball continues to march down the field when, in humility, you ask forgiveness from various key players in your life.

The first step in seeking forgiveness is confessing your actions to Christ: "If we confess our sins, he is faithful and just and will forgive us our sins and purify us from all unrighteousness" (1 John 1:9 NIV). After admitting any wrongdoing to Christ, then you can approach your loved ones.

Seek forgiveness of your wife. Thoughtfully consider all the ways you have emotionally or physically injured your wife. Ask if she could find it in her heart to forgive you for (*name specific offenses*).

If she does forgive you, thank her. Be careful, however, not to interpret this as readiness for reconciliation. Otherwise, she may view your apology as an act of manipulation or a ploy to get her back. On the other hand, if she says she is not ready to forgive you, then give her the necessary time and space. Tell her that you totally understand her reluctance and that you've obviously caused more pain than you realized.

She may be withholding forgiveness because she isn't convinced that you fully understand what you have done wrong in the past.

Some women have never heard their husbands admit they're wrong. Your wife may be one of them. Admitting your mistake(s), and expressing sorrow for wrongdoing, contributes to the healing process. It's like a 40-yard run, allowing you to maintain possession of the ball for another series of downs. Seeking forgiveness from your wife starts to reopen her closed spirit, and it advances the ball toward the end zone of reconciliation.

Perhaps you ask your wife to forgive you, but you don't get a response. Before you quit, we encourage you to start the process again. Begin with the loving attitude of being soft, and work your way to forgiveness again. Remember, don't just respond to your wife's words. In the heat of battle, she may say something in retaliation to hurt you if you've deeply hurt her. She might respond, "You don't deserve to be forgiven. I really don't know how I put up with you for so long!"

There have been times when I felt something Norma said to me was unfair, even though I was trying to be soft and ask her to forgive me. Perhaps she misinterpreted my motives or questioned my character in the process. When you're asking your wife to forgive you, it's not the time to get into a lecture on the precise wording of the problem. Your focus should be on draining away the anger and not on compounding it.

Remember Jack, the man whose infidelity caused his wife to drive him out of the house? Jack learned quickly that he needed to apply the principles in this book. He started by confessing his sin to God, and he experienced the cleansing that God promises. His dirty slate was washed clean. His all-important vertical relationship had been reestablished. He next needed to restore his relationships at the horizontal level with his wife, kids, family, and friends. He needed to be able to ask for forgiveness from them. Asking for forgiveness from those he'd offended helped to heal the wrong he'd done.

A pivotal play in Jack's reconciliation drive was asking his wife to forgive him for being unfaithful. In brokenness and humility, Jack asked Deanna if she'd grant him the priceless gift of forgiveness. He dropped to his knees and proposed anew to Deanna, asking her if she'd marry him all over again. He renewed his vow to her and to God. He then slipped the ring back onto Deanna's responsive hand. The healing had begun.

Seek forgiveness of your kids. When one player is penalized, the whole team loses yardage. It's no different in a marriage. Your kids have experienced some measure of grief at your hands. Asking your kids for forgiveness is a game-winning field goal. If your kids are old enough to understand (and they're usually "older" than you give them credit for), talk with each child individually, asking each one to forgive you for your not loving his mother as you should have. Ask him to forgive you for not being the father he needed.

Tell the children in age-appropriate ways why the family is separated right now. Explain that your separation or divorce is an adult decision and an adult problem, for which the kids bear no responsibility or guilt. Indicate that it's important for you and their mom to have this time of being apart for a while. Release them from any guilt they may feel for the breakup. Assure them that it is not their fault. Reinforce your love for them.

If your kids are older, realize that they are not immune to the awful effects of separation and divorce. The heart of a child, even an adult child, will be discouraged. You show them value and honor when you take the time to individually share with them your sorrow over this present loss. They don't need to be dumped on, but they shouldn't be left out either.

Seek forgiveness of your in-laws. Effective as a long-completed pass is your asking forgiveness of relatives. Because the ripple effect of separation and divorce is far-reaching, asking forgiveness of key relatives affected may prove beneficial. Jack found this difficult step propelled him forward in the whole process of bringing healing to his wife's deep hurt and, ultimately, to their marriage. He specifically asked Deanna's family to forgive him for hurting her.

A separation or divorce hurts the whole family, immediate and extended members. The grim reality is that grandparents miss their grandkids. Cousins, nephews and nieces, and aunts and uncles are affected. It's just not the same, and everyone may feel uncomfortable at family get-togethers. Tell your relatives that you realize your separation strains the whole family and that you are working on making the needed changes. Acknowledge that they might not be able to trust what you're saying yet, but that they will see your sincerity proven over time. We encourage you to be careful about how you do this. Your wife will quickly get word of your newfound enlightenment and remorse, and she may read the effort as a clever means of recruiting others against her. Therefore, she may throw a penalty flag.[4] If your behavior matches your words, reality can prove itself out—over time.

A genuine attitude is essential when seeking forgiveness.

If you are doing all this to look good or score points, realize that everyone can usually tell this type of action, and you may lose major yardage as a result. On the other hand, when you remorsefully admit your mistakes and seek forgiveness, you are being humble. Having a humble spirit is perhaps the best way to melt your wife's angry and closed spirit. Humility can improve the situation by leaps and bounds. Remember, "God opposes the proud but gives grace to the humble" (James 4:6 NIV).

Your relationship can be restored only through God's grace.

4. Show Genuine Repentance

A reconciliation drive stays alive with this all-important relationship play. The word *repentance* means a complete about-face. It's a change of direction—it's a 180-degree turn. Boston philosophy professor Peter Kreeft describes repentance as threefold:

> It is a matter of the heart, the mind, and the behavior. It is a matter of the heart because the heart is the captain of the soul. It is a matter of the mind because we must "bring every thought into captivity to Christ." And it is a matter of behavior because "faith without works is dead." The will is the captain, the mind is the navigator, and the hands and feet are the engines of our ship. The whole ship needs to turn [repent].[5]

When true repentance occurs, your relationship is able to turn around. In the Bible when the chief tax collector, Zacchaeus, repented of cheating the people, he evidenced remorse through his change of behavior by paying back those he had swindled four times the original amount (Luke 19:1–10). That's saying, "I'm sorry . . . I'm sorry . . . I'm sorry . . . I'm sorry!" When Zacchaeus did that, nobody questioned his heartfelt repentance.

Zacchaeus's story brings to life the heartfelt repentance expected of us all in the book of James:

> Be humble then before God . . . Come close to God and he will come close to you. You are sinners: get your hands clean again. Your loyalty is divided: get your hearts made true once more. You should be deeply sorry, you should be grieved, you should even be in tears. Your laughter will have to become mourning, your high spirits will have to become dejection. You must humble yourselves in the sight of the Lord before he will lift you up. (James 4:7–10 PHILLIPS)

It's one thing to say you're sorry or say you're committed to putting the family first; it's quite another thing to give concrete evidence of your words. Jack gave concrete evidence that he was remorseful by demonstrating obvious changes in his behavior. He dedicated himself to being completely open with Deanna concerning his comings and goings. No more half-truths, partial information, or silent treatment. He stopped saying to her, whether directly or indirectly, that his every move was none of her business.

As a result of his including Deanna, she feels valued, secure, and loved. They keep current with each other—from facts to feelings—and find that doing this keeps their marriage interesting, not stagnant. The by-product of doing a

180-degree turn is that each person can gain a deeper under-standing about the other.

So far, we've looked at the first two steps toward winning your wife back: (1) understanding how nine penalty flags can damage the reconciliation process, and (2) opening your wife's closed spirit. Now we turn our attention to the third step, which is the single most important principle for build-ing healthy relationships.

Step . . . .
Three . . . .

Honor Your Wife and Children

Honor is the cornerstone for restoring and building all relationships—with God, your spouse, kids, friends, boss, and coworkers. Put into action, it works like a thrilling kickoff return. To honor someone is to attach high value to that person. It's a decision we make, regardless of our feelings. Deciding to place high value on our wives or other loved ones can begin to change their feelings toward us. Biblically speaking, we express honor to others by how we talk to them and treat them: "Husbands, in the same way be considerate as you live with your wives, and treat them with respect [honor] as the weaker partner and as heirs with you of the gracious gift of life, so that nothing will hinder your prayers" (1 Peter 3:7 NIV).

You might be thinking, *How can honor help me to win back my wife?* Patricia McGerr wrote a story called "Johnny Lingo's Eight-Cow Wife," which illustrates the unlimited power of treating someone as a valuable treasure.

A long time ago there lived a young islander named

Johnny Lingo. He lived on Nurabandi, not far from the island Kiniwata in the Pacific. Johnny was one of the brightest, strongest, and richest men in the islands, but people shook their heads and smiled about a business deal he had made with a man on Kiniwata. He had paid the unheard-of price of eight cows for a wife, who was by any standards unattractive. As one fellow explained, "It would be kindness to call her plain. She was skinny. She walked with her shoulders hunched and her head ducked. She was scared of her own shadow."

The amazing fact was in those days, two or three cows could buy an average wife, and four or five a highly satisfactory one. Why would Johnny pay eight? Everyone figured Sarita's father, Sam Karoo, had taken young Johnny for a ride, and that's why they smiled whenever they discussed the deal.

The teller of the story finally met Johnny for herself and inquired about his eight-cow purchase of Sarita. She assumed he had done it for his own vanity and reputation—at least she thought that until she saw Sarita: "She was the most beautiful woman I have ever seen. The lift of her shoulders, the tilt of her chin, the sparkle of her eyes all spelled a pride to which no one could deny her the right." Sarita was not the plain girl she had expected, and the explanation lay with Johnny Lingo.

"Do you ever think," he asked, "what it must mean to a woman to know that her husband settled on the lowest price for which she can be bought? And then later, when the women talk, they boast of what their husbands paid for them. One says four cows, another maybe six. How does she feel, the woman who was sold for one or two? This could not happen to my Sarita."

"Then you did this just to make your wife happy?"

"I wanted Sarita to be happy, yes. But I wanted more than that. This is true. Many things can change a woman. Things that happen inside, things that happen outside. But the thing that matters most is what she thinks about herself. In Kiniwata, Sarita believed she was worth nothing. Now she knows she is worth more than any other woman in the islands."

"Then you wanted—"

"I wanted to marry Sarita. I loved her and no other woman."

"But—" she said, close to understanding.

"But," he finished softly, "I wanted an eight-cow wife."

Because Johnny Lingo considered Sarita to be worth eight cows, she began to feel and present herself as an eight-cow woman. Before Johnny entered her life, Sarita was a shy, plain island girl. After he placed incredible value upon her, she was transformed into a confident, attractive woman who knew she was worth far more than any other woman.

More than ever before, your wife might be feeling as Sarita did before she met Johnny. With all the negative events that led up to your wife's leaving, she may feel like a one-cow woman. During this separation time, however, you can give your wife the same gift that Sarita received: incredible self-worth seen through the eyes of someone who considers her priceless. Strive to make your wife understand how valuable she is to you by taking the steps outlined in this book. As you start to see her as priceless, like Sarita, she may begin to feel and present herself as an eight-cow woman. It's plain and simple: honoring your wife is like returning a kickoff 110 yards for a record-breaking touchdown. When this happens, there is no limit to the way she may respond to you.

To honor your wife in your marriage is to treat her as the most important player on the team. She is the franchise player—the object of your cheering. My franchise player or MVP is Norma, whose autographed picture graces my office like that of a champion athlete.

You can honor your mate by telling her that she is equally capable of calling the plays. That means encouraging her to have a say in running the team, listening to her viewpoint, and utilizing the plays she calls. Honoring your mate means protecting her, like offensive linemen forming a wall of protection around their quarterback. In football there are rules designed to protect the quarterback from injury. Honor is the biblical principle God designed to protect each mate from being unnecessarily injured.

When you honor your wife, she will sense that nothing and no one in this world is more important to you. She won't have to wonder if she is number one—she'll know. Love in action will confirm this to her.

After Jack made the intentional commitment to honor Deanna and the kids, they felt important. His loving and thoughtful actions toward them were so strongly demonstrated and so reassuring that his wife felt security for the first time in her life, resulting in her trusting him again. In fact, she says that her trust has grown to the extent that if Jack is ever unexpectedly late, Deanna worries about his safety, not his whereabouts. Honoring your wife and your kids puts feet to the words *I love you*.

Each day I praise God for my wife and her daily growth and failures—as I realize God can turn everything about her into something that's good for me and that glorifies Him. Every day I let Norma know just how special she is and what a privilege it is that I get to be her husband. According to Philippians 4:8, praising my wife is the true and noble and right and pure and lovely and admirable and excellent or praiseworthy thing to do—whether things are going well or whether Norma and I are experiencing conflict.

Last summer, I challenged tens of thousands of Promise Keepers to honor their wives with praise and practical service. The men responded by writing out various ways they planned to honor their wives when they returned home.

One simple way to honor your mate, cited by many of these men, is to regularly show that you appreciate her. Specific words of praise (not flattery) always score major points. Flattery is insincere or excessive praise. Flattery is giving praise rooted in motives of self-interest—that is, it implies you want something from her. Praise, on the other hand, focuses more on character qualities and is not self-serving. Praise shows her the tremendous awe you feel at the privilege of living with an All-Pro.

Though sincere compliments are very honoring, many guys don't give compliments of any kind for one reason or another. You may feel it's too flowery, or you may feel uncomfortable putting feelings into words. Or maybe you just don't think of it. Praise should be flowing freely from your mouth, for it is certainly one biblical distinction of a godly man.

Most Christian men like the sound of the idealized, wonder woman of Proverbs 31. But did you see the way the Proverbs 31 man treats her? Her husband is a man of praise:

Her children arise and call her blessed;
    her husband also, and he praises her:
Many women do noble things,
    but you surpass them all. (vv. 28–29 NIV)

Have you ever thought that praise may be the underlying cause of all the Proverbs 31 woman's fruitfulness? Reinforced compliments work wonders in bringing out the best in others.

If your wife does not seem receptive to praise, appreciation, or compliments right now, then write them down for future reference. Note the way she does what she does, who she is, and what makes her so special from all other women. Sadly, many people never know fully or appreciate deeply what they have until they no longer have it. Purpose today to become the kind of man who regularly gives words of praise by looking for specific character qualities.

You can learn from Johnny Lingo's example. You can make the decision to honor her—treat her as a "ten-cow" wife—even if you no longer share the same bed. Honoring a separated or former wife is treating her with dignity and respect when you have contact with her. Another way of expressing honor to any woman is respecting her boundaries. The fourth-down marker flips over to indicate a first down every time you respect your wife's boundaries or limits.

Honoring Your Wife's "Fences"

In years past I've verbally violated my way into many of my most valued relationships. I was like a tank smashing down the protective and sometimes fragile walls around my wife's and kids' hearts. Even if they wouldn't let me in, I'd say, "I'll come in anytime I want, and you'll like it." Now I'm learning how to knock on Norma's gate first and see if she wants me to visit her concerning something serious, time-consuming, or critical.

People are too precious to jump over their walls without permission. It may cause serious hurt; often we never know how much until years later. Your wife has fences that protect her privacy or need for emotional space. Respecting these boundaries shows her that you honor her requests. These fences are taller and thicker when you are separated—and permanent when you are divorced. These fences may even have the police behind them, for example, restraining orders by the court. In either event, you're to put an honor guard at the opening of your mouth and say only things that build up your wife unless she specifically asks you to say the hard things.

Let her call the shots without always having to explain or defend herself to you. When she says, "I don't want to talk about that right now," drop the issue and ask when would be a better time. If she tells you, "Don't call me or drop by," honor her by obliging her request. Don't counter by saying, "But I love you and want to hear your voice and know how you're doing." Resist telling her, "But you're my wife, and I should be able to call you."

Ask your wife for her parameters regarding how often she would welcome a visit, a call, or a letter. When you repeatedly ignore her requests, you lose possession, figuratively and literally—which is all-important in the game of football and in marriage.[1]

When you decide to put your wife (and kids) above

everything else on earth, you at once plant the seeds of security and hope. Honoring your wife can provide a calming, relaxing effect on her, for it will be meeting one of her greatest needs—the need to feel secure. As an act of your will and in obedience to God's commands, you can decide from this moment on to honor your wife, whether or not you believe that she deserves it. To honor her is always the right thing to do: "Be devoted to one another in brotherly love. Honor one another above yourselves" (Rom. 12:10 NIV).

Another way to win back your wife is found in something that is closely tied to honor. Sacrificial love can help you to do three extremely important things for your wife.

Step . . . .
Four . . . .

Develop Sacrificial Love

You have now seen the importance of understanding nine penalty flags, opening your wife's closed spirit, and honoring her. Closely tied to honor is the next step in the reconciliation process, which is learning how to have sacrificial love. Many years ago I heard a story that helped me to understand the tremendous power of this type of love.

During the summer, my children attended a Christian sports camp called Kanakuk. While they were at camp, the counselors taught them various lessons about God and good sportsmanship, to name a few. My kids' favorite lesson, however, was about the "I'm third" principle because they got to hear the heroic story of an Air National Guard pilot named Johnny Ferrier.

The following story is an account of the most important day in Johnny Ferrier's life, a day that he had been preparing for all his life. This story was written by Ed Mack Miller, entitled "The Man Who Matched Our Mountains," and was featured in the *Denver Post* December 3, 1961:

Out of the sun, packed in a diamond and flying as one, the Minute Men dove, at nearly the speed of sound, toward a tiny emerald patch on Ohio's unwrinkled crazy quilt below.

It was a little after nine in the morning of June 7, 1958, and the target the Air National Guard's jet precision team was diving at was famed Wright-Patterson Air Force Base, just outside Dayton, Ohio.

On the ground, thousands of faces looked upward as Colonel Walt Williams, leader of the Denver-based Sabrejet team, gauged the high-speed pullout. For the Minute Men pilots, Colonel Walt Williams, Capt. Bob Cherry, Lt. Bob Odle, Capt. John Ferrier, and Major Win Coomer, it was routine, for they had given their show hundreds of times before several million people.

Low across the fresh green grass the jet team streaked, far ahead of the plane's own noise. Judging his pull-up, Colonel Williams pressed the microphone button on top of his throttle: "Smoke on—now." Then the diamond of planes was pulling straight up into the turquoise sky, a bushy tail of white smoke pluming out behind the formation. The crowd gasped as one, then the four ships suddenly split apart, rolling to the four points of the compass and leaving a beautiful, smoky fleur-de-lis inscribed on the background blue of the sky. This was the Minute Men's famed "flower burst" maneuver. For a minute the crowd relaxed, gazing at the tranquil beauty of the huge white flower that had grown from the lush Ohio grasslands to fill the great bowl of sky.

Out on the end of his arm of the flower, Col. Williams turned his Sabre hard, cut off the smoke trail, and dropped the nose of his F-86 to pick up speed for the low-altitude cross-over maneuver. Then, glancing back over his shoulder, he froze. Far across the sky to the east, John Ferrier's plane was rolling. He was in trouble. And his plane was headed right for the small town of Fairborn, on the edge of Patterson field. In a moment the lovely morning turned to horror. Everyone saw, everyone understood. One of the planes was out of control.

Racing his Sabre in the direction of the crippled plane, Col. Williams raised his normally calm tone on the radio: "Bail out, John. Get out of it." There was still plenty of time, still plenty of room. Twice more Williams issued the command. "Bail out, Johnny—Bail out!" Each time he was answered by a blip of smoke. He got the sense of it immediately. John Ferrier couldn't reach the mike button on the throttle because he had both hands tugging on a control stick that was locked in full-throw right. But the smoke button was on the stick, and he was answering the only way he could—squeezing it to tell Walt he thought he could pull out . . . that he couldn't let his airplane crash into the houses of Fairborn.

Capt. John T. Ferrier's Sabrejet hit the ground midway between four houses. There was hardly any place other than that one backyard garden where he could have hit without killing people. There was a tremendous explosion which knocked a woman and several children to the ground. But no one was hurt—with the exception of Capt. Ferrier. He was killed instantly.

Major Win Coomer, who had flown with Ferrier for years, both in the Air National Guard and on United Air Lines, and had served a combat tour with him in Korea, was the first Minute Man to land at Patterson AFB after the crash. He got a car and raced to the crash scene.

He found a neighborhood still stunned from the awful thing that had happened. But there was no resentment as is ordinarily the case when a peaceful community is torn by a crash. A steady stream of people came to Win Coomer who stood still in his flying suit, beside the smoking, gaping hole in the ground where his best friend had died.

"A bunch of us were standing together, watching the show," an elderly man told Coomer, "when he started to roll. He was headed straight for us. For a second I felt that we looked right at each other." There were tears in the man's eyes. "Then he pulled up right over us and put it in . . . there." And, humbly, he said: "This man died for us."[1]

It was a bold and courageous last act. But it was not an act alien to the nature of John Ferrier. He had been awarded one of the nation's highest medals for risking his life "beyond the call of duty" in Korea. Although he didn't know it, he had been preparing for that day all his life. Johnny Ferrier spent his life practicing one of the most important principles in life: sacrificial love.

Johnny Ferrier died so that others might live. This is a

great lesson you can also learn during this time of separation. This lesson is outlined in Ephesians 5:25–33 (PHILLIPS), where Paul diagrammed a surefire relational first-down play, with X's and O's (husbands and wives) in their proper roles and functions. He pointed to the husband, saying, "The husband must give his wife the same sort of love that Christ gave to the Church, when he sacrificed himself for her."

Not only did Christ sacrifice Himself for the church, but He allowed Himself to be nailed to a cross so that we could have eternal life. You need to learn how to sacrifice in that way for your wife. If you find yourself saying, "Well, Jesus was able to make that kind of sacrifice because He is God; that really doesn't apply to me," we want to encourage you to realize that not only can you make the ultimate sacrifice, but you need to learn how to do this on a daily basis for your wife and children. Sacrificial love says that you honor others above yourself. Paul went on to write, "Men ought to give their wives the love they naturally have for their own bodies . . . Let every one of you who is a husband love his wife as he loves himself." He was not suggesting that you roll over and play dead. He meant that your wife's happiness is your first concern.

As a husband, you are not commanded to merely love your wife. Instead, you are instructed to love her a certain way—sacrificially. The word *sacrifice* is rarely used these days other than in baseball (sacrifice bunt or sacrifice fly), advertising (the loss leader), or missionary circles. Scripture exhorts a husband to lay down his life (forgo your own agenda) that his wife might advance (her career interests, her ministry goals, her security needs).

Like Johnny Ferrier, Coach John Wooden understood this

all-important principle, incorporating it into both his personal life and his professional life. He gave this principle lasting value when he made it one of the building blocks for his famous Pyramid of Success. He defines *team spirit* as "an eagerness to sacrifice personal interests or glory for the welfare of all. The team comes first."[2] Every marriage is a team of two. To exhibit and enjoy team spirit, you must have an eagerness to sacrifice personal interests.

Eager to sacrifice—that means preferring your wife above everything on this earth. "Do nothing from selfishness or empty conceit, but with humility of mind let each of you regard one another as more important than himself; do not merely look out for your own personal interests, but also for the interests of others" (Phil. 2:3–4 NASB). As the verses point out, genuine love is forever asking the question, "What do you need me to be or do?" not, "This is what I need from you!"

Preferring each other is God's game plan for a winning marriage. Christ calls the man to love sacrificially, and when you are sacrificing, it will feel like it because by definition, sacrifice is a sacrifice. It means giving up something you want to hold on to for something else, and that loss is real and that loss is felt. The truth is, loving your wife sacrificially may hurt more than crashing an airplane for her because it hits the area that is most precious to you—whatever that is.

This call to love sacrificially is not a one-time sprint for the end zone as the game clock runs out. There are opportunities every single day to express this kind of love, even when you're separated or divorced. Specifically, we encourage you to do three important things that can show your wife sacrificial love.

1. Become a Servant

Jesus said, "The greatest among you will be your servant" (Matt. 23:11 NIV). What a powerful statement! If you want to be considered "great" to your wife, then we suggest you start by learning to become a servant. Anytime you promote her program or agenda over yours—without grumbling or complaining—you sacrificially love her. Allowing yourself to be inconvenienced for her qualifies as sacrificial love. When you invest your time for her, without keeping score, you are loving sacrificially. It may mean something as simple as switching cars with her. It may hurt worse—missing out on an important family gathering because your presence would add a strain to the occasion. It may mean forgoing your vacation plans this year or paying a bill for a debt you didn't incur. It may be letting her have the kids during "your time."

When the family is reunited, you communicate sacrificial love in the following ways:

- Watching a program she'd like to see.
- Eating where she prefers.
- Forgoing ESPN Sports for a night, so you can talk with your family.
- Living where she has always wanted to.
- Buying the car she is comfortable with.
- Getting dressed up when you don't feel like it.
- Heading to the mall with her when it's the last thing you feel like doing.
- Not hassling her about sexual frequency or performance.
- Spending more time with the kids on a regular basis.

These are great ways to communicate how much you value serving your wife. Think of several specific things you could do for your wife to show her sacrificial love. Remember that it does not qualify as a sacrifice unless it really is one.

2. Contribute Financially

Continuing to financially support your wife and kids works like a breakaway 60-yard run! This area is vital because very few things express love more loudly than a man's providing for his home. Conversely, nothing shouts indifference quite like a man's withdrawing his support. Consider this strong admonition of Paul: "If anyone does not provide for his own, and especially for those of his household, he has denied the faith and is worse than an unbeliever" (1 Tim. 5:8 NKJV). Worse than an unbeliever! Nobody wants that reputation. But that's what God thinks, and so may your wife. Love is not just something you say; it's also something you do. Providing financially is doing the loving thing by giving sacrificially.

This whole area of finances presents a major stress point for all concerned. Some gallant (but untrusting) men we know would sooner take a bullet for their wives than sign a paycheck over to them. If you now find yourself out of your home, it's important to bend over backward to show that you can be trusted to provide and care for your family financially. This ranks as one of the most important things to which you can commit yourself because your hard-earned money paves the way between you and your wife. Giving of your finances shouts volumes to your wife. She receives the message that you will do whatever it takes to show that you're learning what true love means. It also says much about your character—that you're sorry and that you still care. It says that you're responsible and that you can be depended upon. But most important, it shows L-O-V-E in capital letters!

However, do not expect overwhelming thanks for providing for your family. If you do, your wife may suspect that you're trying to bribe her. Some wives refuse any monetary help whatsoever, especially if they feel that it has come to them with strings attached—it buys time with them or the kids, or it imposes guilt on them to reconcile. Your wife may refuse financial assistance from you because she does not want to be obligated to you, be indebted to you, or feel dependent on you in any way. Tell her that you understand her feelings and that you'll check back with her at a later date to see if your help would be appreciated. If child support is court ordered, you have a legal obligation to fulfill this financial duty, and anything you do beyond this scores major points.

Helping with expenses can speak deeply to your wife. It may unlock the door to negotiations, inclining her to hear what you have to say. But don't fall into the money-for-kids negotiation trap to which some courts and many couples succumb. In other words, if you are in the middle of a court settlement or one appears imminent, this whole area of finances will prove to be your greatest test of character. Fairness should be everyone's objective. Naturally, no one wants to be taken to the cleaners. But fighting over "things" hurts people. You can determine the distribution of assets and liabilities by continually submitting your property division and child support endeavors to a simple test. Ask these questions:

- Is it the truth?
- Is it fair to all concerned?
- Will it build goodwill and better friendships?
- Will it be beneficial to all concerned?
- Are love and honor the base for all my motivations and actions?

Although this can be a very confusing and stressful time to be thinking about money, look for creative ways you can sacrifice in order to make provision for your family. Ask the Lord for ideas and then be alert to His leading.

3. Offer Additional Help

In addition to financial assistance, we encourage you to ask your wife about what kind of help she and the kids would welcome during this stressful time of transition. Maybe you have no more money to offer, but you have the time to take the young children more often, thus alleviating the need for expensive day care. Perhaps you could provide more of the transportation to and from doctor appointments and extracurricular events. Is there anything you can do or provide if the house needs maintenance? If your wife senses no hidden agenda, she may very well disclose needs and welcome your help.

As you become a servant to your wife and family, contribute financially, and offer additional kinds of help, you will be showing her the type of sacrificial love that Christ Jesus has called us to exemplify. Next, we will be dealing with four personal areas that might need to be changed if your wife is to reconcile with you.

Step . . . .
Five . . . .

Initiate Change in Yourself

Another way to move the first-down chain forward is to initiate change in yourself. A tough marine drill sergeant learned about the importance of making changes. He got word that the grandmother of one of his men had died, and at reveille he barked, "Hey, Wilson, your grandmother died!" The young soldier fainted on the spot.

A few days later the grandfather of another marine died. The sergeant once again called the squad together. "Peterson," he shouted, "your grandfather died this morning!" The soldier wept as he heard the news.

Finally, word got back to the commanding officer about the drill sergeant's insensitivity. He was confronted about his behavior and told to change. Specifically, the sergeant was instructed to be less direct and gruff when one of his men suffered a tragedy.

Several weeks later the sergeant was notified that Private Walters's grandmother just passed away. Remembering what the commanding officer had ordered, he lined up his troops.

"Everyone whose grandmother is alive, please take one step forward. Not so fast, Walters!"

Like the drill sergeant, you can constructively use this time of separation to make changes and improvements in your life. If you are a workaholic or alcoholic, get help—today. Find balance. Spiritually lukewarm? Plug back into Christ. If you're having an affair, break it off at once. Trust is the cornerstone of the institution of marriage. Once the trust stone crumbles, it's difficult to rebuild. Nothing shatters it all to pieces quite like adultery. New trust can and will have to be constructed. But the construction is not swift or easy.[1]

If you need to make changes, we encourage you to make them now. Your wife will probably not live with the same man she left. She left because of some problems. If you are having difficulty determining areas in which you need to grow, ask your wife for a list. If she is unwilling to help you, ask several of your close friends. Your wife is not waiting for you to attain a sanctified, glorified state of perfection. However, she is looking for integrity, honesty, health, and balance.

Personal Growth in Four Areas

"Jesus increased in wisdom and stature, and in favor with God and men" (Luke 2:52 NKJV).

Here we find a beautiful example of balance—growing mentally, physically, spiritually, and socially. It is helpful to inventory your life according to these areas.

1. Mental
What exercise is to the body, reading is to the mind.

Consider this convicting axiom: "The person who doesn't read is no better off than the person who can't read." The disciplines of reading and writing sharpen the mind. There are enrichment classes, seminars, and programs that promise to stimulate and equip your mind. Here's a checkup from the neck up, to answer on your own:

- Are you mentally fit or intellectually stagnant?
- Are you always learning, renewing your mind, and taking in new information?
- Are you up to date with what's happening in the world?
- Have you made yourself interesting by being interested in what's going on around you?
- Are you developing and feeding any "software" (resources) into your "hardware" (your mind)?
- What was the last book you read? Video series you watched? Seminar you attended? Series of tapes you heard?
- Do you feel comfortable being able to discuss a wide range of topics?

If you answered no to several questions, or many of these do not apply to you, then you should spend more time reading and learning.

2. Physical

One evening a husband slammed down a book he was reading and stared intently at his wife. "I'm through sitting around here with you all the time," he shouted. "I want to find someone I can have fun with. I'm going to shower, shave, and use some of that cologne I just bought. I'll put on my best suit. After that, I'm coming back down here, and guess who's going to knot my new silk tie for me?"

His wife slowly glanced up from her magazine and replied, "The undertaker?"

Perhaps your wife feels like this woman—she can't take you seriously when you say you're going to get dressed up and take her out on a date. Maybe your wife makes jokes because it has been a long time since you made your appearance a priority. If you can relate to this, here's a checkup from the neck down, to answer on your own:

- Are you physically healthy, in playing shape, or are you more of a couch potato?
- Are you taking good care of yourself, or is someone taking care of you?
- Are you free of all addictions (smoking/drinking/drugs/food/sex/pornography/gambling)?
- Are you current with medical and dental checkups, or could you not care less?
- Is your outward appearance a source of confidence, or is it a source of embarrassment? Is it neat and clean, or is it offensive and disheveled?
- Are you open to wearing what your wife suggests?
- Do you participate in any physical activity that relieves tension and stress?
- Do you smell good to your wife? Do you wear her favorite cologne?
- Does your physical appearance communicate "I love you" to your wife?

If you answered no to several of these questions, think

about making changes in this area. Showing concern about physical appearance communicates honor to most women.

3. Spiritual

A husband gains immeasurable yardage when he is committed to this area. If your wife craves a godly home and husband, to touch this area affects the deepest part of her. Consider this checkup from the inside out:

- Are you advancing spiritually, or would the Lord tag you "spiritually lukewarm"?
- Is your knowledge of God growing deeper (Col. 1:10)?
- Are you in the position to assume spiritual leadership in your home?
- Do you include the Lord in your decision-making process?
- Are you a man of prayer?
- Do you regularly read your Bible?
- Do you faithfully attend church?
- Do you naturally discuss spiritual themes in your home?
- Are you a "Sunday-only Christian" or a consistently committed one?
- Are you a man of integrity? A man who walks the talk?

If you responded negatively to several (or many) of these questions, remember that nothing touches the soul of a Christian woman more deeply than when her Christian husband prioritizes the spiritual aspect of his life. There is hardly anything more attractive to a wife than seeing her husband kneeling in prayer or having an open Bible on his lap. Most women love praying with their spouses and discussing spiritual matters together.

"So because you are lukewarm, and neither hot nor cold, I will spit you out of My mouth" (Rev. 3:16 NASB). This verse poignantly explains that spiritual lukewarmness sickens God and can quickly sicken a Christian marriage as well. Neglecting this area exposes your wrong priorities to your wife and seriously jeopardizes any hope of reconciliation.

Jack successfully kept possession of the relationship ball by reprioritizing this key area of his life. He became regularly involved in church and didn't leave his spirituality on the church steps each week. He became a spiritual presence in his home. Jack and his wife pray together now on a daily basis. He kneels at the kids' bedsides to pray with them each night. As a result, he continues to advance spiritually, and his spiritual growth is a deep source of pride for his wife.

4. Social

Now let's turn our attention to the last vital area in which to initiate change. Perhaps socially, you feel like the man who was walking with his wife in the park. The couple noticed two lovers sitting on a bench, passionately kissing.

"Why don't you do that?" said the wife.

"Dear," explained her husband, "I don't even know that woman!"

If in the past you have misunderstood your wife's romantic hints or have become boring over the years, make changes in this area. Here's a checklist that will help you examine the social dimension of your life:

- Would your wife say you are social or antisocial?
- Are you considered a people person or a hermit?
- Do you and your wife regularly do things with others?

- Do you plan outings and events for the two of you to enjoy together?
- Is your family making special memories that your kids will take with them all their lives?
- Do you make plans to do the things your wife enjoys doing with you?
- Are you truly enjoying life?
- Do you resist attending social functions because of cost or the trouble it takes to get ready?
- Do you welcome others into your home?
- Do you balance work and fun?
- Do you mingle with people or hurry away after an event?

If you've answered no to many of these questions, you might have a deficit in your social life. Too many women complain that after a few years of marriage, the fun stops. They used to enjoy playing with their mates, but now that's all a fading memory. Responsibilities have crowded out the fun they used to have; everything is serious and routine. Bills. Job. Kids. Errands. Maintenance. Life.

A husband in the diligent pursuit of balancing these areas is an exciting turn-on to his wife. But be confident that balancing the physical, mental, spiritual, and social areas is an important pursuit regardless of your marital status.

We've looked at five steps for you to take in order to win back your wife: (1) understand how penalty flags can damage the reconciliation process; (2) open a closed spirit; (3) honor your wife and children; (4) develop sacrificial love; and (5) initiate change in yourself. All of these first-down plays can help you score points to narrow the gap between separation and reconciliation. In the next step, we encourage you to begin understanding three reasons why some women are unable to accept efforts at reconciliation.

Step . . . .
Six . . . .

Understand Why Some Women Are Not in a Position to Reconcile

his step requires extra sensitivity. And it's possible that some readers will be tempted to file all their marital problems in this one drawer. We encourage you to resist the urge to do so. This is not a catchall drawer for you to use as the reason that you and your wife are not together. It might be tempting to declare, "Well, no wonder nothing I do works! Nothing could ever work with her. *She* is the problem!"

This step can be useful only if you have successfully incorporated everything else we've outlined—and your wife still remains unresponsive. If that is the case, then we suggest you closely examine three areas for possible explanations of her behavior. They may or may not help you understand why your wife resists your efforts. Because people are complex, they may not fit into nice little boxes of explanations. These areas are worth considering, however, and worth your prayers.

Some women have so much emotional baggage they are hauling around from past relationships that almost nothing their husbands do will make a significant difference in the relationship today. Some women must hurdle major barriers before reconciliation can occur.

If your wife is imprisoned by her past, it does not mean that your marriage is a hopeless situation or that you should stop efforts to reconcile. It just means that further digging by a counselor and your earnest prayer are required so that all transgressions against her life can be cleared away. Think of it in terms of a word picture. The ground must be prepared before anything new can be planted. It must be hoed, raked, and watered. Your wife may need to work through major areas to be able to receive love from you.

If your wife's soil has hardened, she may not allow your changes, improvements, or efforts to impact her. A woman is not in a favorable position to reconcile if she is struggling with her past or with an addictive behavior. She may have suffered a mental breakdown and is not prepared to take on a reconciliation attempt. Sometimes you are severely limited in what you can do or communicate until she receives specialized help.

Linda was that type of woman. She met her husband, Frank, when she was only sixteen, and they quickly became high school sweethearts. Soon, Frank began to pressure Linda to become sexually active. As a result, after only two months of dating, Linda became pregnant. At first, Frank seemed content with their decision to keep the baby and get married. Since Frank was a senior, he was able to finish high school and get a job. Linda dropped out of school to become a full-time mother. Because of a job offer, Frank moved his new family several states away from Linda's parents. Although Linda felt very alone and isolated, the first several months of marriage were fairly good. As with most couples, Linda and Frank had their disagreements, but nothing ever got physical—at least not right away.

Linda will never forget the day Frank first laid a hand on her. They had been arguing about finances when out of the blue, Frank grabbed Linda by the throat and slammed her head against the kitchen wall. The sheer force of the blow literally left an impression in the wall. Linda was terrified. *What is happening?* she desperately thought. *What have I done to provoke Frank like this?*

Later that night Frank explained that he was not used to women disagreeing with his decisions. "I don't want any lip from you!" were his exact words. Linda cried herself to sleep that night. It would not be the last time.

Over the next few months, Frank became extremely demanding and jealous. Linda was required to meet his every desire. Whether it was for her to stay up with the baby or to comply with unwanted sexual advances, Linda had to obey, or she would receive a "reminder." Sometimes Frank's reminders consisted of pulling her hair or slapping her across the face. But most of the time Frank's abuse was vicious. Linda continually had dark bruises over her face and body. After the beatings, she usually justified Frank's behavior as being her fault—as if somehow she had brought it on herself.

After the birth of their second child, Frank's behavior worsened. At different times Frank awakened Linda at two in the morning because he was hungry. He forced her to go out and bring back some food. They had been married more than two years. Linda was starting to develop major physical side effects from his violence, not to mention the psychological problems accompanying such abuse. She was deeply depressed and often considered ending her life. *How did I get myself into this?* she thought repeatedly.

The children were her only reasons to live. But she could see no way out. Because of the tremendous negative effect of Frank's abuse on her self-esteem, Linda believed that she could not survive on her own. She was a prisoner in her own home.

Finally, Linda's break came. Frank had recently been laid off at work, and the family was struggling financially. To help make ends meet, Frank demanded that Linda take a part-time job at a church near their home. Through the support of church members, Linda got up the courage to leave Frank. But it wasn't going to be easy—Linda knew that Frank would not let her and the kids simply leave.

She vividly remembers the day that she planned to leave. It was on a Friday because Frank would be hunting with a friend, spending the weekend in the mountains. Linda had made plans to stay with some relatives in California. They agreed to let her and the kids live with them for a few weeks until Linda could get a job and her own apartment. The plan was perfect—or so it seemed!

Linda spent Friday night packing the car because she was going to leave at the crack of dawn Saturday morning. It was difficult for her to sleep that night. It seemed to last forever. Morning arrived, and Linda scurried around to finish the last-minute details. Unfortunately, it took longer than she'd planned to get the remaining items and the kids into the car. It was almost 8:00 A.M. She had to get out of the city. Once she and the children were on the road, she knew that everything would be okay. Linda was so nervous that she could feel her heart thumping with every beat.

Linda felt more relaxed as she backed the car out of the

driveway. However, her nightmare would not end so easily. Because of bad weather in the mountains, Frank and his friend had decided to cancel the hunting trip.

Linda and the children hadn't gotten half a block away when Frank's truck suddenly came around the corner. Linda was terrified. *Frank will kill me if he sees me trying to leave*, she thought. She started to panic as the adrenaline surged throughout her body. She quickly prayed, "Lord, please help us get away!"

As Frank's truck approached, Linda knew that at any second he was going to run them off the road. *What's this?* she thought as a glimmer of hope surfaced. *Frank isn't driving!* Miraculously, Frank was sound asleep in the passenger's seat, and his buddy did not recognize her as they drove past each other. Linda was free to start a new life.

My son, Greg, was amazed at Linda's story when he first heard it during their counseling session. He remembers repeating the word *unbelievable* several times throughout the story. By the time Linda came to see Greg, she had been divorced from Frank for several years. She had met a new man, and they wanted to get married. They decided to seek premarital counseling in order to work through some of Linda's issues that were affecting their relationship.

The first thing that Greg explained to them was that Linda's fiancé might have difficulty meeting some of Linda's needs. Because of the abuse, no matter how sincere an effort her fiancé made, sometimes Linda would not be able to respond as he needed. It took the couple a solid year of premarital therapy before they built the necessary foundation they needed to have before they could get married. The good news is that because they remained in counseling and worked extremely hard, they were able to construct a wonderful relationship.

Similar to what happened to Linda and her new husband, as you attempt to rebuild your marital relationship, many of the things you do may be met with resistance from your wife. We encourage you not to become discouraged; instead, realize and accept that it may take many months or years to break through the walls of resistance and reconcile your relationship. Specifically, we want to discuss three reasons why some women react negatively to a man's sincere efforts.

1. Some Women Have Been Victimized

Linda's story is a helpful reminder that if your wife has suffered physical, mental, or verbal abuse at your hands, she may well resist your sincere efforts at reconciliation today. She may come to the place of forgiving you, but her mind will never erase the frightful memories. That she is now reluctant to trust you again should not be a surprise. Remember the principle we previously discussed: the greater the hurt, the longer the healing time. For some women it might take a lifetime. Therefore, keep doing the positive things you should be doing, but allow your wife plenty of time to heal. You do not help matters by becoming anxious or pushy.[1]

If your wife was abused by one of her parents—especially her father—she may still be responding to that trauma years later unless she has received specific help in that area. If her father was an alcoholic, was angry or distant, rejected her, committed incest with her, walked out on the family, or just wasn't there for her, chances are, the image of that man has been sleeping between you and your wife.

A woman who was abused and has not found healing or restoration may sabotage her relationship with you. If a woman is really locked into the pain of the past, she may provoke you by various means so that you treat her in a dishonoring way.

Why? Though being lonely or rejected feels bad, it is more familiar and feels more comfortable than feeling loved or unconditionally accepted. Anger that's buried deep inside from the past can act like a wall between the person and the one she is trying to love. Also, the fear of being hurt again by anyone can keep her from moving closer to you.

This is no doubt very frustrating and discouraging to a husband who is trying to make a fresh start by doing all the right things to honor and value his wife. These serious problems don't go away on their own. Pray that she will avail herself of the specialized help she needs. Pray that she finds a loving support group and gifted counselor to help her work through her issues so that she will be free to receive your love. Pray that she finds the wisdom of someone like Dr. David Seamands, who gives many secrets of being healed from the past in his book, *Healing for Damaged Emotions*, or help from my own book, *Joy That Lasts*, dealing with this issue.

2. The Personality Bent Affects Responses to Life

Because of their superior abilities in building meaningful relationships, some women make light of a man's attempts to relate meaningfully. They criticize or minimize sincere efforts. Some are forever suspicious whenever a man shifts gears from ram tough to bunny soft. Some women are such perfectionists that no measure of performance will satisfy them. These are obvious brick walls to hurdle, and until their hearts are softened, they may not let their husbands in.

Another natural tendency, which can serve as a barrier to reconciliation, has to do with personality types. Each of us has a personality bent, and we respond to life in accordance with it.

Some personalities, pushed to an extreme, tend to be hard on people. These types are not as inclined to give second and third chances when a separation occurs. They live in a black-and-white world, with little or no shades of gray. Everything is either/or for them. Other personality types lean toward the soft side of relationships. These people feel it is only fair to try again. Different temperaments handle tension in different ways. Therefore, if your wife has resisted your efforts at reconciliation, understanding her personality type can provide additional insight into why this is happening.

One way to categorize personality bents is to describe them using the four animal types that Dr. John Trent and I talk about so often in our books: (1) the lion, (2) the beaver, (3) the otter, and (4) the golden retriever.

The Personal Strength Survey

In each box, put a check mark next to every word or phrase that describes a consistent character trait of yours. Total the number checked in each box, then double your score. Next, take the total score from each box, and mark it on the chart. Once you complete the survey for yourself, fill it out for your wife. Put a star next to every word or phrase that consistently describes your wife's character traits. Take a few minutes now to complete the survey and fill in the graph before continuing. On the graph, use dots for your marks and stars for your wife's marks.

Lion
"Let's do it now!"

Likes authority	Productive
Takes charge	Bold
Determined	Purposeful, goal driven
Confident	Decision maker
Firm	Adventurous
Enterprising	Strong willed
Competitive	Independent, self-reliant
Enjoys challenges	Controlling
Problem solver	Persistent
Action oriented	

Otter
"Trust me! It'll work out!"

Enthusiastic	Takes risks
Visionary	Motivator
Energetic	Very verbal
Promoter	Friendly
Enjoys popularity	Fun-loving
Likes variety	Spontaneous
Enjoys change	Creative
Group oriented	Optimistic
Initiator	Mixes easily
Infectious laughter	

Golden Retriever
"Let's keep things the way they are."

Sensitive feelings	Loyal
Calm, even keel	Nondemanding
Enjoys routine	Dislikes change
Warm/relational	Gives in
Indecisive	Dry humor
Adaptable	Sympathetic
Thoughtful	Nurturing
Patient	Tolerant
Good listener	Peacemaker
Avoids confrontations	

Beaver
"How was it done in the past?"

Accurate	Consistent
Controlled	Reserved
Predictable	Orderly
Factual	Conscientious
Perfectionistic	Discerning
Detailed	Analytical
Inquisitive	Precise
Persistent	Scheduled

Personal Strength Survey Chart

	"L"	"O"	"G"	"B"
40				
30				
20				
10				
0				

After you've determined scores for both you and your wife and have transferred the scores to the chart, what does it all mean?

Lions are take-charge leaders. They are decisive, bottom-line people who are doers, not watchers or followers. They're not afraid of confrontation. They're not afraid of anything. Lions want immediate results and their time frame is *now*.

Beavers, on the other hand, have a strong need to do things right and by the book. Their lives are orderly. There is a place for everything, and everything is in its place. Rules, consistency, and high standards are very important to beavers. They like to make careful decisions and tend to focus on the past.

Otters are fun-seeking, excitable, cheerleader-type people who love to talk. They are parties waiting to happen! These people are outgoing and great motivators. The focus of otters is usually on the future. Furthermore, they tend to want to avoid confrontation because it's no fun.

Golden retrievers are a "loyal 'til the bitter end" kind of people. They can absorb emotional pain and punishment in relationships. They're helpers and pleasers, even a one-person support team. These people usually have a strong need for close relationships. Finally, golden retrievers are full of compassion, and they exemplify the word *adapt*.[2]

You might be wondering what this information possibly has to do with your wife's resisting your reconciliation efforts. Actually, it can have a lot to do with your situation. When a personality bent is not in balance, then it tends to be either too hard or too soft. In a separation or pending divorce that will translate this way: the lion and beaver personalities will tend to be more critical of reconciliation attempts. A husband will have to do more in order to prove himself. It will be more difficult to patch things up, though not impossible. Those with an otter and golden retriever bent tend to be too soft and will sometimes tolerate behaviors that should not be tolerated. Sometimes their weakness will keep them in an abusive relationship, even if it's dangerous. They may give repeated chances to reconcile, whether or not the needed changes have been made. Generally speaking, lions and beavers grant second and third chances less freely. On the other hand, otters and golden retrievers will almost always try to make the marriage work in various ways.

3. Their Spirits May Be Closed to Anger

Although we extensively dealt with this issue in step two, it's worth saying one more time: unresolved anger in your home is more toxic than poisonous gas! When anger coats a relationship, it hardens the heart, making it unyielding.

Anger can also produce low self-esteem. A victim deeply feels low self-esteem. As a result, if your wife is a victim, she may long for affection, but resist being treated with tenderness or consideration. A woman can harbor anger left over from everyone who has hurt her in one way or another. She may have unresolved anger from hurt you've caused her. Her spirit will be tightly closed to you if you have not taken the necessary steps to open her spirit by seeking forgiveness. You will never be successful in your most important relationships until you learn how to drain the anger out of another's life where you have been the primary contributor. Reuniting with someone full of anger is very difficult.[3]

Some women have emotional baggage they are carrying

around from past relationships. Because some women have been victimized, have a particular personality style, or have a spirit that is still closed, it may seem that nothing their husbands do makes a significant difference in the relationship. Some women must conquer these major hurdles before reconciliation can occur. As a result, you may become very disheartened because nothing you do seems to work with your wife. This is precisely the reason for the next step.

Step seven can help you to picture the situation: your wife never comes back and yet you still win the game. We will show you how to find hope in your loss and faith in your future.

Step ....
Seven ....

Understand the Ultimate Goal
When Your Wife Leaves

T he ultimate goal of our lives is to draw closer to the Lord. Your wife's leaving can be a powerful push that moves you toward the arms of God. Knowing Him and letting Him be your strength and your joy are worth the pain it takes to drive you into His presence. This lesson was very difficult for Dave to learn.

Although today Dave is a man of God, he would be the first to tell you that his path to godliness has been paved with pain. He has suffered deep heartache. One of the most serious, crushing blows knocked out his marriage.

After fourteen years of marriage he found himself in the middle of an opportunity to enrich his character if he responded properly to a huge trial. His marriage was in trouble—again. He had already weathered several marital storms throughout his and Laura's relationship, and the latest one looked as if it would be the final storm to capsize their once "love boat" marriage. Dave knew things were bad; they had been for years. Sex was nonexistent. He gave up expecting it—ever.

The waves crashing against their relationship were towering and forceful. He knew his wife's childhood had been difficult, with a dysfunctional family. She harbored deep anger toward her parents. Her unresolved anger had taken up full-time residence in their home as well as in her heart. Laura had been unfaithful to him on more than one occasion.

Dave wanted to stay married. He cringed at the thought of starting over again—alone or with someone else. But he also knew that things had to change.

Dave began to pray and believe that his relationship could be saved, and he also began to take the steps we've outlined within the pages of this book. Dave held on to the hope that his marriage would be healed. Sad to report, Dave and Laura never reunited, but Dave took the opportunity to grow closer to God through his painful experience.

As Dave had to learn, regardless of how desperately you want to win back your wife, your number one goal should not be to win back her affection, noble as that is. It should be to become a man after God's own heart, a man of God. The goal is to become the kind of man that God stands ready to help you become—regardless of your marital status.

Your ultimate goal is to become an effective, fervent, and righteous man who glorifies God in all you do and say, and to be committed to pleasing God rather than men.

You will want to emulate the qualities mentioned in Psalm 112. A godly man fears the Lord and will be remembered forever. He loves God's Word and puts his trust in the Lord. He is a gracious, compassionate, affectionate, and generous man.

He is secure and knows his true wealth resides in the Lord, not in his bank account.

Dave's family and friends will testify that his life bears strong witness that though he lost his marriage, he emerged a victor. Because Dave chose to receive this trial as an invitation to grow in humility and in love, the end product of that decision wonderfully reflects the promised reward. Dave asked his Redeemer to do what only He could do—make something worthwhile and valuable out of what lay in ruins.

Dave's life today is marked by maturity, keen insight, godly wisdom, humility, and discernment. Today his family, his friends, his peers, and his community admire him. His life gives evidence that your present sorrow—if not wasted through bitterness, resentment, or anger—can produce a mature character and a hope that will never disappoint you. That's the promise of Romans 5:3–5 (NIV): "We also rejoice in our sufferings, because we know that suffering produces perseverance; perseverance, character; character, hope. And hope does not disappoint us, because God has poured out his love into our hearts by the Holy Spirit, whom he has given us."

Dave committed himself to many of the things we have talked about. He tried valiantly to win back his wife, but it was not to be. Nevertheless, he found God more than faithful. You guard against grave disappointment when your motivation for change is God's glory and not the express purpose of winning your wife back, thus avoiding divorce.

We encourage you to make three very important commitments. The first is to grow closer to the Lord, the second is to gain an understanding of why your wife left (or asked you to), and the third is to practice humility.

1. Make a Commitment to the Lord.

It is impossible to become a man of God without God! Therefore, it is important to commit or rededicate your will and ways to the Lord. In support of this, Paul made an interesting observation about the Macedonian Christians that applies to us today. In 2 Corinthians 8:1–5 (NIV), Paul described the generous and giving nature of the Macedonians:

> Now, brothers, we want you to know about the grace that God has given the Macedonian churches. Out of the most severe trial, their overflowing joy and their extreme poverty welled up in rich generosity. For I testify that they gave as much as they were able, and even beyond their ability. Entirely on their own, they urgently pleaded with us for the privilege of sharing in this service to the saints. And they did not do as we expected, but they gave themselves first to the Lord and then to us in keeping with God's will.

The explanation Paul provided for their willingness to give was that since their relationship with God was on target, they were able to give beyond the limits of their means. The picture of the Macedonian Christians reinforces that our vertical relationship with God dictates our horizontal ones with people. In Paul's words to the Christians at Ephesus he noted, "Make it your aim to be at one in the Spirit, and you will be bound together in peace" (Eph. 4:3 PHILLIPS).

This is not to guarantee that as you move nearer to God, your wife will automatically move in with you or even closer to you. On the contrary, Paul was saying that unity breeds harmony, that peace is a bond, and that regardless of your marital status, both of you can enjoy a peaceable state.

Mike's story underscores this principle. During their wedding ceremony, Mike and his wife pledged to love each other until death. But they joined thousands of other couples who first signed a marriage certificate and then divorce papers. The breakup of his marriage, however, was the catalyst that brought Mike back to a closer walk with the Lord.

Purposing to be at peace with the Lord, Mike knew he could not harbor ill feelings toward his wife. But that was easier said than done. After several years of marriage and putting his wife through college, she came home one day and announced, "You've been a dynamite husband and a wonderful provider, but I'm leaving." To add insult to injury, Mike's wife eventually moved in with a guy from their gym. Her decision to do her own thing meant that Mike would now be forced to also. His plans for having a family and growing old together with his wife were suddenly gone. He found himself sobbing until he couldn't take it anymore.

His only alternative was to turn it all over to the Lord. Within twenty-four hours he was flooded with peace he never realized was possible. He was freed of all inclination to judge or blame her. Two months later they met, and his ex-wife immediately sensed Mike's newfound peace and freedom. His presence so impacted her that it drained any awkwardness or defensiveness from her. She finally gave her life to the Lord as well!

As it turned out, they ended up working at the same place and attending the same company meetings and events. They can converse in the halls without feeling strained. Mike is at peace with God and with his ex-wife. The Lord has replaced all ill feelings for her with genuine care and concern. The situation could have been ugly, but it wasn't.

Mike's attitude changed toward his ex-wife because he followed Paul's admonition to prioritize the spiritual relationship before the earthly ones. Your commitment to God needs to precede your commitment to your wife. It sets the tone for everything else you do. You cannot get to point B (where you want to be, the goal line) without first identifying point A (where you are now, first down with 80 yards to go). God has a specific game plan mapped out for your life: He is the Alpha and the Omega, the Beginning and the End; hence, your spiritual relationship with God dictates all other relationships.

Pray, Pray, Pray . . . Read, Read, Read

Humility is valuable when making a commitment to God, and equally vital is the role of praying and Scripture reading. Like Mike, ask God to keep you from all temptation, especially the temptation to blame. Ask Him for wisdom, direction, and guidance so that you'll know what to do and what not to do. Pray for the desire to do the right thing and the ability to accomplish it. Seek His help to take away all bitterness, resentment, and anger, and to replace them with His strong love shown in wonderful ways. Pray that the Lord will reveal where you have been wrong and where you have failed to show honor.

Ask Christ to reveal what your wife needs, where she is hurting, and how she is hurting. Seek His help to identify with her pain and understand your wife better. Ask Him to help you become the man He longs for you to be.

We encourage you to pray for the openness to learn—then wear out your Bible. Scripture is called a lamp to your feet and a light to your path (Ps. 119:105). Reading the Scriptures on a daily basis provides guidance in this sin-darkened world. Regularly turning its pages is like turning on the stadium lights for a night game. It can help you see what you're doing. Think of the Bible as a rule book for all of life and for every relationship. A wise man will familiarize himself with this all-important manual.

When you love God's Word, He promises to grant you great peace. You will also gain wisdom, understanding, discernment, and moral purity. You need all these qualities on your team.

Two-Point Conversion

Perhaps you've come to the point in your life where you recognize you've been calling all of your own plays. You're at the place where you can now admit that your game plan for life needs divine assistance. The Head Coach, God almighty, stands ready to step in and help you if you'll just ask Him. The Bible tells us that we all blow it and fall short of the goal (Rom. 3:23). We all need forgiveness for our sins.

If you have never committed your life to Jesus Christ, your conversion is set in motion when you (1) by faith, trust in the fact that Jesus Christ is the Son of God and the Savior who came to reconcile us to God the Father; (2) admit you lived a self-centered and sinful life against God; and (3) pray, inviting Jesus Christ to be the Lord of your life.

When you make that decision, it's as if God turns on the "microphone" inside your "helmet" so that you can hear Him speak directly to you. He gives you the gift of the Holy Spirit to guide and direct you. He also gives you the Bible, which is His playbook, and it's filled with His truth. (Look up

John 10:3–5; 2 Cor. 9:8; Phil. 4:13, 19; Col. 1:9–11; 1 Peter 2:1–2; Rev. 3:20.)

2. Gain Understanding

Another important commitment is to acquire understanding. We encourage you to commit to gaining clear knowledge of why your wife left (or asked you to). If you are on speaking terms with your wife, ask her this question that will get you back in the game: "What miracle would have to happen before you would be willing to consider reconciliation?" Take notes while you carefully listen to her response. This question can be very valuable during this time because your wife is giving you the exact things that you need to do to bring about reconciliation.

No one knows better than she why you and she are separated. Therefore, no one knows better than she what it would take to reunite. You need to be able to clearly identify and articulate the reasons for your marital difficulties. If you need help identifying areas of neglect, abuse, or dishonor, you can ask family and friends what they have witnessed about your behavior that troubles them. Scripture tells us that the wise man seeks counsel: "Through presumption comes nothing but strife, but with those who receive counsel is wisdom" (Prov. 13:10 NASB).

Another way to look at this is to consider how much preparation goes into every football game. Think of all the input (counsel) obtained by the coaching staffs on both sides. They pore over detailed scouting reports and endless statistics, review game films, and lay out strategies. Hours of dialogue and fact gathering transpire in order to gain a vivid picture of the opponent to be played. The head coach and his assistants wouldn't dream of entering a game without the confidence that they are fully prepared.

Seeking individual counseling may help you review the game films of your life. The counselor can act as a personal scout, pointing out your strengths and weaknesses. An objective therapist can help you gain understanding into issues that rained down upon your wife and family through the holes in your relationship umbrella. The therapist can help you patch (heal) those holes in the relationships.

Some men will react negatively to the suggestion of seeking individual counseling. This may be a result of our cultural stigma, which says that men who ask for help are admitting inadequacy. Fortunately for us as husbands, the reverse is true. The Bible tells us that plans fail for lack of counsel, but with many advisers they succeed (Prov. 15:22).

Asking outsiders for input and insight into your life isn't easy or fun. In fact, it's often painful because it lies outside your comfort zone. But like any required surgery, it's the very process that brings about healing and wholeness. Do whatever you can to understand the factors that soured your marriage. If that remains a confusing or cloudy issue, then growth from this experience may be stunted, and any future relationship may be adversely impacted.

If you do not come to fully understand what went wrong in your current relationship, then you risk putting yourself in the unenviable position of repeating the same mistakes. Be open to learning all you possibly can, from every source available to you. Enroll yourself in the classroom of life, gaining both the knowledge and the skills to interact meaningfully. Become a student of relationships. Every single day of your life is a relationship "lab," providing countless opportunities to improve and excel in this all-important area.

Resist the temptation to resort to blame. Refuse to tell your wife, "You're the one who needs help," or "You're the problem here." Be very diligent, but not hasty, in your pursuit to find the reason(s) why your marriage is in its current state. Being solution oriented may cause you to miss significant factors that may or may not be obvious.[1]

A man who seeks counseling and applies what he is learning gains valuable yardage. Where is the inadequacy in that? Women attach high value to a man seeking counsel. Your wife may interpret this move as a step toward gaining understanding, owning responsibility, and getting needed help. It shows humility to her, a teachable spirit, and that instills hope in her heart for you and for the marriage. This leads us right into the third commitment to make during the reconciliation process: the practice of humility.

3. Practice Humility

Another essential aspect of making a commitment to Christ is humbling yourself in His sight. When your wife left, a pivotal timeout was called, and all action ceased. We hope you will use this timeout to go directly to the Head Coach, God, and listen to His instructions. This is the essence of being humble. When you go to someone for help, you admit that you do not possess the answers or solution.

The good news is that this Head Coach calls every play perfectly. He'll tell you what He wants you to do and won't mind repeating Himself because He delights in showing you the way: "The Lord is good and glad to teach the proper path to all who go astray; he will teach the ways that are right and best to those who humbly turn to him. And when we obey him, every path he guides us on is fragrant with his lovingkindness and his truth" (Ps. 25:8–10 TLB).

Confess to Him the behaviors or attitudes that you know have grieved Him. Ask Him to forgive you and set you on your feet once more. That was where Jack started his reconciliation drive. His marriage comeback with Deanna began by first repenting of his sin to God. What God had joined together, Jack had torn asunder by his infidelity. He humbly asked God to forgive him for breaking his marriage vows and asked God to bring healing to his marital relationship.

The road to wisdom and true prosperity is entered through the door of humility. Pride, in any measure, jams that door. A proud man shuts himself off from what he desperately needs: God's help and favor. When you humble yourself, God floods you with all the help you need. He promises to lift your spirits and comfort you.

The Bible has much to say on the subject of humility:

Humble yourselves, therefore, under God's mighty hand, that he may lift you up in due time. (1 Peter 5:6 NIV)

Whoever humbles himself will be exalted. (Matt. 23:12 NIV)

This is the one I esteem:
   he who is humble and contrite in spirit,
   and trembles at my word. (Isa. 66:2 NIV)

Okay, suppose you've managed to avoid the penalty flags and you've been able to string together successive first downs, but time is running out and your wife still refuses to reunite. Now what? The answer is found in step eight as illustrated by a word picture that Jesus painted for His disciples in Luke 18.

Step . . . .
Eight . . . .

Never Give Up!

One of the most powerful things that I have discovered in life is found in Luke 18. It's a story about how we should pray for one another. The word picture that Christ used is about a widow who never gave up standing in front of a wicked judge. She kept asking every day for protection against people who were stealing from her.

Imagine an unrighteous, wicked judge assigned to a small city in Israel. He has no respect for God or man. He is disgruntled because he would rather be in Rome enjoying pageantry, games, and parties. Instead he is stuck with a bunch of farmers, shepherds, and religious fanatics. Every day people line up to present their grievances to him, and he passes judgments according to his mood.

In the line of people stands a widow with no one to look out for her best interests or to protect her. Her situation appears hopeless. Others take advantage of her because she has no legal rights. Although many look at her as helpless, she knows the secret to gaining justice. The first time she presents her petition to the judge, he abruptly dismisses her. But she does not give up. After many days of standing in line, she finally receives protection from the wicked judge.[1]

"Why did the wicked judge grant this woman her request?" Jesus asked. "Because she wore him down!" Jesus concluded by telling how much more our heavenly Father gives us when we stand in line every day with our prayer requests.

What Jesus talked about is what you can do during a difficult time of reconciliation. Jesus said to listen carefully to the story of this unrighteous judge. He depicted an important truth people need to understand: the woman's persistence brought results. Jesus went on to say, "And will not God bring about justice for his chosen ones, who cry out to him day and night? Will he keep putting them off? I tell you, he will see that they get justice, and quickly" (Luke 18:7–8 NIV).

Like the widow, you need to persistently stand before the Lord each day—asking if today is the day He will answer your prayers. You must never give up asking the Lord to bring the needed improvements and growth necessary to help in this process. Continue to ask God for the wisdom, the insight, and the strength to keep going. Never give up!

You can continue to wait upon the Lord until He renews your strength. He will cause you to rise up and fly like an eagle, walking and not fainting. Why? Because He will do it in His time, especially when it's His will. Strong, vibrant relationships are His will. If that isn't true in your marriage, you can continue to pray for it.

Near the end of his life, Winston Churchill was asked to give a commencement speech at a noted university in England. His car arrived late, and the jam-packed crowd suddenly hushed as one of the greatest men in British history made his way slowly, painfully to the podium. Churchill's speech lasted less than two minutes—but it drew a standing ovation at the time and has inspired decades of men and women ever since. What he said is the best advice you can receive when it comes to being persistent in the face of obstacles.

What did he say? With his deep, resonating voice, he said only these twelve immortal words: "Never give up . . . Never, never give up . . . Never, never, never give up."[2] Then he sat down.

Few can appreciate Churchill's message quite like Jim and Jessica. For them, "never give up" means far more than a positive rallying cry or a historic speech. It is the testimony of their marriage experience, which they now feel called to share with others.

The best of friends, Jim and Jessica became husband and wife in the spring of 1975. Back then they sat for hours together and talked about everything. The only subject they discovered that brought any level of tension was church attendance, so they never mentioned that topic again. They got along great and enjoyed being a couple.

To spice up their marriage, Jim thought up games the two of them could play together. One of these games involved going to a bar, pretending not to know each other, getting picked up, then going home together. It seemed innocent enough. But the game soon lost its excitement for Jim. Slowly, Jim allowed other toxins to poison their marriage. Wanting to please her husband, Jessica allowed what she thought she never would—Jim brought other women home with her approval. Yes, this sickened Jessica, but she was too weak to offer any resistance to this damaging activity. Not only did she allow other women into her home, but more and more lies came through the door. Some time later, Jim informed Jessica that he was leaving her for another woman, but only for a few months to get it out of his system. Completely devastated, Jessica found temporary relief in a liquor bottle.

Jim's temporary separation stretched into a permanent lifestyle of going from one woman to another. Jessica filed for divorce, which was devastating for her. That was when the Lord brought a strong Christian friend into Jessica's life who shared the good news of Christ's forgiveness and unconditional love. Jessica invited Jesus into her life, and the healing process began.

Divorced for a year and a half, Jessica still had contact with Jim. Grateful for the work the Lord had begun in her own life, she began praying earnestly that Jim would come to know Jesus personally. Jessica invited him to come to a free concert her church held on Wednesday evenings.

Two thousand people attended the concert that night, but Jessica was in earnest prayer for only one. At the end of the service, with all heads bowed, the pastor called forward those who desired to accept Christ as their personal Lord and Savior. Jessica felt someone brush past her. When she looked up, Jim was making his way to the front of the church! Through tear-blurred eyes, Jessica watched Jim drop to his knees and confess his sins. A floodgate of tears opened up, and Jessica wept so hard, she could barely breathe.

Did Jim and Jessica patch things up that night and live happily ever after? Hardly. Remember, theirs is a story of persistence.

Jessica continued to grow as a new Christian, while Jim

learned the hard way to depend on Jesus alone for life's fulfillment. Six months later Jim had lost his latest girlfriend, his job, his house, and his cherished '57 Corvette. It had been three years since Jim and Jessica had separated.

Having faced significant loss, Jim was a broken, now genuinely repentant man. Slowly, he and Jessica began seeing each other again. They attended church and went to marriage counseling. Feelings returned as a result of their new decision to love each other as God had intended. A new foundation of trust was poured. And to the glory of God, Jim and Jessica were remarried in the winter of 1989!

Jim and Jessica want everyone to know that there is power in persistent prayer. They want to shout to everyone, "Never give up!" The steps to their enjoying a reconciliation and remarriage are the same ones that have been outlined in this book. Jim repented and made his spiritual life his top priority. He joined a men's fellowship group, and he is still being held accountable. Likewise, Jessica has been working on her issues and has been learning along the way. She has discovered what it means to put God first, not her husband.

God is still closing the gap between what soured their marriage and what has now sweetened it for them. Theirs is a story of hope. This hope is delivered to your address by such encouraging words as, "Anyone who is among the living has hope" (Eccl. 9:4 NIV).

There Is Hope

If you're alive and breathing, you can have hope! The psalmist had hope and hung on to it: "I will hope continually, and will praise Thee yet more and more" (Ps. 71:14 NASB).

And what about the powerful testimony of Israel's founding father, Abraham? He, too, faced a major test of his faith. God promised to build a great nation from his descendants, yet his wife was barren. What did Abraham do? "Against all hope, Abraham in hope believed" (Rom. 4:18 NIV).

How was he able to do that? The rest of that passage sheds light on the answer. It says he relied on the word of God (v. 19). He refused to distrust what God had told him (v. 20). He gave God the glory (v. 20). He remained absolutely convinced that God was able to do what He promised (v. 21).

By definition, faith is being confident of things we cannot see (Heb. 11:1). We can hope in the middle of a hopeless situation because the object of our hope is God Himself. Out of His strong love for you He has generously provided promises sufficient to meet your every need: "My God shall supply all your need" (Phil. 4:19 NKJV).

Is God able to restore your relationship? In Joel 2:25 (NIV), He promises to "repay you for the years the locusts have eaten." Can He revive a dead marriage? We read in Luke 1:37 (NIV) that "nothing is impossible with God." Can God make something good out of something awful? God promises to give "beauty for ashes . . . joy for mourning . . . praise for the spirit of heaviness" (Isa. 61:3 NKJV).

Many have found comfort in what God has promised His people in the face of adversity:

He gives strength to the weary
    and increases the power of the weak . . .
Those who hope in the LORD
    will renew their strength.
They will soar on wings like eagles;

they will run and not grow weary,
they will walk and not be faint. (Isa. 40:29–31 NIV)

May you find the same strength of the Lord as you run with perseverance the race now set before you.

Let's Review

At this point, we have looked at the importance of understanding how penalty flags damage reconciliation, opening a closed spirit, honoring your wife and children, learning how to have sacrificial love, initiating change in yourself, understanding why some women are not in a position to reconcile, understanding the ultimate goal when your wife leaves, and maintaining persistence as you struggle to win back your wife and family.

Someone told us recently that Moses wandered in the desert for forty years because he refused to stop and ask for directions! We have consistently mentioned that seeking advice and wise counsel is indispensable during this difficult process. As authors, we agonize over the thought of putting one of the most important steps in the last part of the book. Although it fits here logically, the concept shared in the next step is vital to every man who wants to win back his wife, as well as to every family and church across our world.

In the next step, you'll discover the most powerful way we know to infuse encouragement, motivation, and even positive correction into a person's life. Without this next step, you may start to feel trapped, wandering aimlessly in the desert of marital despair.

Step . . . .
Nine . . . .

Be Accountable by Joining a Support Group

One proven method of stimulating personal growth and making important improvements in your life is putting yourself in a position of loving accountability. This isn't putting yourself on the chopping block where someone will cut you off at the knees. Rather, accountability means letting someone be close enough to your life that he can ask you the really tough questions.

As men, we need our brothers to keep us on the straight and narrow, so we do not slip back into old habits and patterns of behavior. We encourage you to get some people in your life who care enough to confront you and who will also be there to provide moral and prayerful support.

If you've ever participated in a long-distance run, you know the adrenaline boost you get when you hear a group of roadside fans shouting your name and cheering you on. That's what personal accountability can be for you—a major morale booster. In the race of life, there is a variety of effective and beneficial ways to solidify godly principles and strengthen a couple's relationship, for example:

- Join a men's small group study.
- Ask a mature believer to mentor you.
- Attend a Promise Keepers conference and follow-up group.
- Participate in a Homes of Honor interactive video program by Gary Smalley.

We Need One Another

Left to yourself, you may slide back to your old ways. Having regular contact with other men and/or couples can help you stay on track. You can't be held accountable for areas in your life unless you let someone get close enough to know what to ask and look for. When a man puts himself in a position of spiritual and relational accountability, this absolutely softens a woman's heart and encourages her in his direction.

An accountability group is vital because it can provide you with many benefits. In the book I coauthored with Dr. John Trent, *The Hidden Value of a Man*, we list these specific benefits gained from a support group:

- Self-control over unwanted habits and thoughts
- Loving support through hearing words of praise, through appropriate and meaningful touch, and through words of hope
- Higher motivation to do what's right
- Dramatically increased self-worth
- "Reparenting" for closeness

- Healthy independence
- Increased life span and decreased susceptibility to sickness
- The resources, reassurance, and perspective of others[1]

Deanna's heart continued to soften toward Jack when he voluntarily joined a men's small group. It was yet another way he could show her that he meant business about becoming the spiritual leader of their home. The men would hold him accountable in his pursuit of godliness. As he became more comfortable with them, he opened up more of his life to them. It was an important day for Jack when he openly confessed his sin of infidelity to his accountability group. Honesty is contagious, and that level of vulnerability and openness has brought all of the men closer together. In addition to this small group, Jack augmented his spiritual fitness program by becoming involved in the Promise Keepers movement. Jack is now a promise keeper, and Deanna is benefiting as a blessed promise reaper.

In your accountability or support group, it can be helpful to have structure around the questions you ask one another. We encourage you to use questions like these:

- Have you spent daily time in Scriptures and in prayer?
- Have you had any flirtatious or lustful attitudes, tempting thoughts, or exposed yourself to any explicit materials that would not glorify God?
- Have you been completely above reproach in your financial dealings?

For additional questions and a deeper discussion of their

meaning and purpose, refer to Rod Handley's book, *Character Counts—Who's Counting Yours.*[2]

In the next step, we invite you to look more closely at what a woman needs in general and what you can do to understand what your wife needs in particular. She is watching carefully to see if you are learning how to take care of her and the kids, and she is watching to see if it's really safe to try again.

Step . . . .
Ten . . . .

Understand Women: The Scouting Report

This scouting report on women shows areas of need, desire, and general inclination. These observations are based on my marriage to Norma, surveys of hundreds of women through the Love Is a Decision seminars, and my niece's ministry with men and women. There may not be much that surprises you because you could learn these same principles by attentively studying your wife.

What we offer here, much like a good pregame scouting report or half-time pep talk, is designed to increase your desire and ability to win at relationships. Furthermore, the goal of this scouting report on women is to help you better understand and appreciate the woman you married. The material is brief (much like a coach's half-time speech), so you can get an overview of what your wife needs.

Conflict Isn't Always Negative

Many wives think as long as you can talk about problems,

the marriage is working. On the other hand, many husbands think the moment you have to start talking about problems, the marriage is in trouble.

We must add a cautionary, but encouraging comment. The presence of conflict doesn't necessarily mean problems, and the absence of conflict doesn't reflect that you are problem free. A certain amount of tension is healthy. Consider a basic camping tent. You need a certain amount of tension between the poles, stakes, and canvas to keep it up. Tension is absolutely necessary for the tent to function as it was designed. However, with too much tension, the whole thing will snap; without enough tension, the same tent will sag.

In relationships you need to find the sensitive balance of tension. Therefore, do not be threatened by the presence of conflict, but use it as a flashing road sign that gets your attention to do whatever's necessary to resolve it. Women want to talk through the problems of the day. Most men would rather avoid the whole thing altogether. As with everything, balance is needed, and it takes both sides working together to achieve it.

Survey Says . . .

The hundreds of women surveyed in the writing of this book provided these important responses.

Asked to list what they value or cherish in a man, the women gave these top five answers:

1. He is a growing Christian and spiritual leader.
2. He has a sense of humor and is fun to be with.
3. He is a man of integrity and completely honest.

4. He is tender, gentle, and sensitive.
5. He prioritizes his family above his work or others.

The same women were asked to answer this question: "If you had the attention of every man around for ten minutes what advice would you want to impart?" They offered these top four responses:

1. Be tender, kind, and gentle with your wife.
2. Listen to your wife—don't cut her off.
3. Have open communication, and share your feelings with her.
4. Spend time with your family, value each one, and make them a priority.

A 3-Point Field Goal to Beat All

What most men don't realize—until they listen—is that they have one of the world's greatest relationship instructors under their roofs. Every woman has an innate desire for a good, healthy relationship. She has within her the natural ability to recognize a healthy relationship, in addition to knowing what can sustain one. In the past thirty years of counseling and speaking all over the world, I have seen firsthand how God has gifted women to intuitively know which relationship plays work best. God has placed inside every woman a playbook, or marriage manual. The wise man taps into this gold mine of relational skills.

I have interviewed more than forty thousand women and have seen this natural ability time and time again. A wise and loving God said, "It is not good for man to be alone." Did

God mean that a woman was designed solely to provide her husband with companionship—or is there a deeper meaning?

Many reading this book are familiar with the passage that references God's creating woman: "I will make a helper suitable for him [Adam]" (Gen. 2:18 NIV). The Hebrew word for "helper" literally is defined as "completer." This word is used throughout the Scriptures to communicate that God is our "helper," the One who "completes what is lacking" or "does for us what we cannot do for ourselves."[1] If a husband wants to know what's best to do in the relationship, he can ask his "helper" or "completer" because she probably knows the answer. That's the way God has uniquely designed and gifted her.

For men who are on good speaking terms with their wives, we suggest three questions that score big with the wives we know. These three questions will help you tap into your wife's built-in playbook. When a man regularly inventories his marriage with this simple three-point exercise, it works like a sudden-death, game-winning field goal every time.

However, for men who find themselves with the door closed to any personal communication about what went wrong in the marriage, we suggest looking closely at questions two and three. Whether or not you have open communication, we strongly encourage you to memorize this three-question relationship tool. It is very likely you will someday find yourself in the position to regularly use it. You can also use this exercise with any person to whom you want to draw closer (e.g., kids, family, employees, business partner)—just change the word *marriage* to *relationship* or something similar.

Question 1: On a scale from 1 to 10, with 1 being terrible and 10 being a great marriage, where would you like our relationship to be most of the time?

Question 2: On a scale from 1 to 10, overall where would you rate our marriage today?

Question 3: As you look at our relationship, what are some specific things we could do over the next six weeks that would move us closer to a 10? (Concentrate on one or two at a time.)

Almost every woman knows the answers to these three questions; however, she needs to feel safe and relatively free from your anger in order to answer them. Patiently and lovingly sharing in this exercise can improve your relationship on the spot. And regularly taking inventory by asking these questions will keep your relationship growing and satisfying. A word of caution: a woman tends to rate her marriage lower than her husband does. Therefore, do not react to her answers or become defensive. Her answers are true for her. Consider each response a gift of honesty that can help you further your pursuit of becoming a mature man of God. Thank your wife for that.

The real value of asking these questions is found in question three. It doesn't matter as much how she scores number two because as she answers the third question, both of you can work together in moving the relationship closer to a 10. By asking question three, you enlist her cooperation in determining the exact things that help to solve your marital problems.

Four Things That a Woman Needs and Her Husband Can Give

What a woman needs is not a secret hidden for the ages or a mystery too tough for a man to comprehend. What a woman needs isn't a Caribbean cruise or an expensive shopping spree. It's to feel deeply loved by her mate. But for her to experience those feelings of love, certain needs must be met. A woman has four areas of need that can make her feel deeply loved. When a husband applies these four ingredients to his marriage, it has the same effect as providing sunlight, water, fertilizer, and air to a plant.

If you work at cultivating the following four areas of your marriage, you will most likely experience a healthy, thriving relationship. (The exception usually comes when there is too much buried anger within either of you.)

1. Unconditional Security

A plant must have sunlight if it's to be healthy and flourishing. In marriage, providing a deep sense of security for your wife is like bathing her in warm sunlight. Every enduring marriage involves an unconditional commitment to an imperfect person. Providing security convinces your wife in a variety of ways that, no matter what, you'll always be there to care for her.

A strong sense of security is an essential prerequisite for a healthy relationship. Your wife desperately needs to feel safe with you. What increases security in a relationship?

- Saying "I love you" regularly.
- Making long-range plans with her.

- Cultivating a pattern of truthfulness.
- Valuing her thoughts and feelings.
- Demonstrating a strong commitment to Christ and to the spiritual health of your family.

When you don't do these things on a regular basis, the weeds of insecurity can sprout and overtake your beautiful plant. Insecurity browns out the leaves of your marriage and dries up the soil. The soil becomes hard and cracked and unable to be tended. Therefore, for the husband who wants to spray lifesaving weed killer on his relational garden, we encourage you to start incorporating some of these security-building behaviors into your daily life.

2. Meaningful Conversation

A plant needs sunlight to grow, but it also needs water. In a marriage, meaningful words bring life-giving water to the soil of a person's life. In fact, all loving and meaningful relationships need the continual intake of the water of communication, or they simply dry up. Communication problems are consistently a major reason for divorce in marriages today. (Financial problems vie for top billing, but financial problems are compounded when a couple cannot talk about them!) No marriage can survive without communication.

When I ask women, "How much time do you need in meaningful conversation each day to feel really good about your relationship with your husband?" the answers are surprisingly similar. The average woman states that she needs at least one hour a day in intimate conversation to keep her marriage alive, thirst-free, and growing. (As each plant is different, you will want to ask your wife how much time she needs in conversation with you to feel really good about your relationship.) A woman needs to feel "connected" to a significant person. Words spoken and heard are the actual fibers that connect a woman to her husband. Words are the key.

Before you panic, however, realize that the hour per day does not have to be spent in a single block of time. Fifteen minutes in the morning as you're getting ready for work, five minutes on the phone from work, twenty minutes after work, fifteen minutes once the kids are in bed, five minutes before bed—that all adds up to an hour.

Meaningful and healthy communication is the lifeblood of love. A relationship will be only as good as its communication. Author John Powell believes this to be "the secret of staying in love."[2]

Every woman wants and can't get enough of communication. But communication is not just something women benefit from. It equally profits every man to become skilled in the art of communication. Communication is the tool of every trade. It's one of the most important skills in all of life. The more effective a man becomes at communication, the higher up the ladder of life he climbs. Yes, women are masters of it, but men can certainly learn to be.[3]

3. Emotional/Romantic Bonding

Every healthy plant needs good soil in which to grow. Likewise, expressions of love fertilize the soil of every healthy relationship. Expressions of love honor your wife and provide the basis for a meaningful sex life. One of the most common reasons why romance dies in a relationship is that it gets inseparably linked with physical intimacy. Though effective romance may sometimes lead to intercourse, its goal shouldn't be sex. Effective romance is not mere foreplay; it's friendship. Men tend to be turned on sexually by seeing women, but women are more turned on because of the friendship and the touch.

Romance is an intimate friendship, celebrated with expressions of love reserved only for each other. And as each plant is different, what is romantic to one may not be romantic to another. It's important to discover what your wife considers to be romantic. For one, flowers will do; for another, it's a late-night jog together. But rarely does romance just happen—and if you wait for perfect conditions, it will probably not happen. Romance springs from thoughtful planning.

Romancing your wife is not something that only newlyweds do. It continues to be a necessary element throughout your married life. When you marinate your marriage in romance, your relationship may never lose its flavor.

4. Positive Physical Touching

To survive, a plant also needs air. Nonsexual touching provides the air for your wife. As we've stated previously, numerous studies have shown that 70 to 80 percent of a woman's physical need is nonsexual. That is, a woman places a higher premium on being held and caressed than on the act of sex. Every area of a woman's life is affected if she is not touched and held by the most important people in her life. On the average, a woman's minimum daily requirement is eight to twelve meaningful touches a day: hugging, patting, stroking, or massaging in nonsexual ways.

A woman needs to experience unconditional security, meaningful conversation, and romantic bonding (the first three needs) in order to respond to this last need for touch.

Meaningful touches outside the bedroom can light sparks inside the whole marriage, and meaningful communication will fan the flame.[4]

We've looked at four of your wife's deepest needs, and you may be excited to learn how to apply these ideas, but some separated wives will be unable to accept any loving gestures because of their deep level of pain. Be patient with your wife. Allow her plenty of time to respond to these things. The information presented here is designed to help you understand the scouting report on what most women need in a relationship. Although you can start applying most of the concepts we discussed, your wife may not respond to you for some time. Once reconciliation takes place, you need to use this information. But for now, you need to put into place a specific game plan.

We have presented all ten steps, and it's time for you to create your own strategy for winning your wife back. Next, we will help you formulate a written, tailor-made plan for immediate implementation.

Write Your Game Plan for Reconciliation

Now that we have covered the ten steps for winning your wife back, it's time to write your individual game plan. The plan you will construct involves three distinct parts. The first part is to determine where you want your marital relationship to be someday and then to gain a realistic view of where it is today.

The second part is to identify what has not been working in your attempts at reconciliation thus far, and discontinuing those behaviors. In other words, find out what is not working, then quit doing those things. It's that simple.

The third part of your reconciliation plan is to identify what things or behaviors have been particularly effective, and continue doing more of the same.

Once you have your reconciliation plan in place, we encourage you to read a good marriage book that will expound on the information we presented in this book. (Several are listed in Appendix B.)

What Type of Relationship Do You Want?

On a scale from 0 to 10, with 0 being terrible and 10 being a great marriage, where would you like your relationship to be most of the time?

Terrible   Average   Great
0—1—2—3—4—5—6—7—8—9—10

Where Is the Relationship Today?

On a scale from 0 to 10, overall where would you rate your marriage today?

Terrible   Average   Great
0—1—2—3—4—5—6—7—8—9—10

Identify What Hasn't Helped—Do Less of It!

As you look at your relationship, what are some specific things you could stop doing over the next few weeks that would move you closer to your goal? Mark the following negative behaviors or penalty flags that you need to stop using with your wife and family.

___ Recruiting others against your wife.
___ Blaming your wife or others for the marital problems.
___ Using dishonoring (critical) speech with your family.
___ Being impatient if your wife does not respond (or slowly responds) to your reconciliation efforts.
___ Setting a time frame for your wife to return.

____ Initiating unwanted physical displays of affection.
____ Overkilling with flowers, cards, and gifts.
____ Underestimating the hurt you've caused your wife and family.
____ Disregarding your wife's boundaries.

For the penalty flags that you marked, review how to discontinue doing these things found in step one. Write out the specific details that will help you stop these destructive behaviors.

I, _____, intend to do the following in order to stop these damaging behaviors:

Recruiting:

_____

_____

Blaming:

_____

_____

Having a critical spirit:

_____

_____

Being impatient:

_____

_____

Setting a time frame:

_____

_____

Displaying affection in physical ways:

_____

_____

Overkilling:

_____

_____

Underestimating hurt:

_____

_____

Disregarding boundaries:

_____

_____

In addition, we have discovered several everyday behaviors that can keep the relationship ball behind the line of scrimmage. Place a check mark before each of the following actions that typified your marriage in recent years. All of us lose ground from time to time and fumble the ball. However, it usually takes five positives to offset one negative. As you mark the ones you are doing, make a commitment to terminate the behavior(s). Then use the list to occasionally review whether you are inadvertently doing any of these destructive things again.

___ Turning on the TV or the computer while tuning out your wife.

___ Being sarcastic with her.

___ Ignoring or degrading her advice or opinions.

___ Criticizing her family and friends.

___ Overcommitting yourself to outside interests.

___ Talking to her or treating her as though she were a child.

___ Living a double standard (doing things you won't allow her to do).

___ Using profanity or name-calling.

___ Letting things go around the house; ignoring her honey-do list.

___ Letting your eyes wander to other women.

___ Criticizing the way she does things (housecleaning, child rearing, etc.).

___ Giving looks of disgust.

___ Raising your voice in anger.

___ Showing more attention to other people than to her.

___ Giving your wife the silent treatment.

___ Correcting her or being rude to her in public.

___ Pressuring her.

___ Lecturing her.

___ Ignoring her.

___ Honking the horn at her.

___ Breaking promises.

___ Making comments about women on TV or in magazines that make her feel inferior.

___ Holding resentment about something she did.

___ Coercing her into an argument.

___ Not trusting her.

___ Being unsympathetic when she is tired, ill, upset, sad, or frustrated.

___ Not telling her that you love her.

___ Not attending church as a family.

___ Demanding that she be involved with you sexually when you are not in harmony.

___ Not being involved with household chores and care of children.

___ Criticizing her womanly characteristics or sensitivity as being weak.

___ Being unwilling to admit when you're wrong.

___ Reading or watching pornography.

___ Being stingy with money.

___ Not eating meals with her.

___ Complaining while doing something with her (having a bad attitude the whole time).

___ Forgetting and/or not celebrating special occasions (her birthday, your anniversary, and Valentine's Day).

___ Minimizing her efforts.

___ Not encouraging and supporting her interests.

___ Being impolite.

___ Wanting to do things that embarrass her sexually.

___ Disregarding her requests to read a certain book, listen to a tape, watch a video, or hear a speaker.

___ Continuing distasteful or harmful habits.

___ Taking her for granted.

___ Being preoccupied with your own agenda.

___ Monopolizing the TV remote control.

___ Blaming her for everything.

___ Being impatient with her: hurrying her to get ready, to finish shopping, or to get to the point.

___ Becoming absorbed in self-interests to the exclusion of her and/or the kids.

___ Kidding or making unkind comments about her body or age (about how she used to look or how much she used to weigh).

___ Questioning her spending.

___ Not consulting or honoring her in decisions to spend/ invest money.

___ Telling her what to do.

___ Taking no time to prepare her for sexual intimacy.

___ Being unwilling to join her in the things she enjoys.

___ Not fully appreciating the mundane and exhaustive chores a wife and mother does (picking up clothes and toys all day, washing, ironing, vacuuming, doing dishes, sweeping, straightening, folding, running errands, making calls).

___ Always showing indifference instead of showing initiative and making plans.

___ Joking about her monthly mood swings.

___ Having an unkempt or unclean appearance.

___ Giving no thought to gifts for her.

___ Physically abusing her (from shoving to beating).

Identify What Has Been or Could Be Helpful in the Reconciliation Process—Do More of It!

As you look at your relationship, what are some specific things you could begin to do over the next six weeks that would move you closer to your goal? Respond to the following eight positive behaviors that you need to start or continue using with your wife and family.

1. Open your wife's closed spirit (if needed, review step two).

I, _____, commit to doing these four things to open the spirit of my wife and children:

    a. Become soft and tender.
    b. Use "drive-through talking" to gain a better understanding of what they have gone through.
    c. Acknowledge that they are hurting, then admit my mistake and seek forgiveness.
    d. Demonstrate genuine repentance.

2. Show honor to your wife and children (if needed, review step three).

We have found certain everyday honoring actions and behaviors that advance the relationship ball and keep possession of it. (Please note that some of them cannot be implemented until you are reunited.)

Since it can take five positives to offset one negative remark or behavior, from the following "honor" list,

I, _____, commit to picking out five or more to use during the next week:

- Regularly say, "I love you."
- Promptly attend to needed household repairs.
- Receive her help without rejecting her or being defensive.
- Call her during the day.

- Share with her my calendar schedule for the coming week/month/year.
- Pray together.
- Show good manners (saying, "thank you," "please," "excuse me," holding doors open, helping her carry things, etc.).
- Know her favorite things and sizes.
- Hug her each and every day.
- Share household chores and do them together.
- Cook together.
- Write little notes to her.
- Give her foot and back rubs.
- Treat her with as much courtesy as I would a friend or even a stranger.
- Kiss her good-bye and hello each day.
- Take her prayer list to work with me.
- Remember birthdays, anniversaries, and other special occasions (celebrate her!).
- Watch her favorite TV program with her.
- Share the control of the TV remote.
- Ask her opinion frequently, and value it.
- Wink at her from across a crowded room.
- Schedule quality time to talk.
- Compliment her often (privately and publicly).
- Make specific family goals for each year.
- Be forgiving when she offends me.
- Plan and initiate fun outings together.
- Show her I need her.
- Plan and prepare a picnic lunch.
- Admit my mistakes.
- Give flowers, cards, or small gifts for no reason.

- Defend her to others.
- Prefer her over others.
- Do not expect her to do activities beyond her emotional or physical capabilities.
- Take time to notice and acknowledge all that she does for me and the family.
- Discipline the children in love, not anger.
- Help her finish her goals (ministry, work, hobbies, or education).
- Get rid of habits that annoy her.
- Hold her hand in public.
- Do not expect a band to play every time I help with the housecleaning or watch the kids.
- Do little things for her (bring her coffee, hold her hand while going up/down stairs, help with errands).
- Treat her as an intellectual equal.
- Take advantage of Valentine's Day to make her feel like the most loved and cherished woman on earth.
- Discover her fears in life and what makes her feel insecure, then see what I can do to alleviate them.
- Ask her how I can better meet her sexual needs.
- Ask if she is jealous of anyone and what I can do to alleviate her suspicions.
- Ask if she is uncomfortable about the way money is spent or invested.
- Honor her thoughts and feelings about how the money is spent or invested.
- Learn to enjoy shopping with her.
- Honor her requests to read a certain book, listen to a tape, or watch a television show or video.
- Take her on weekend getaways.

- Encourage her to spend special time alone and with her friends.
- Have a generous attitude (with my money and time).
- Receive her criticism with humility and gratefulness.
- Be attentive to her—notice what she's wearing, what colors or styles look good on her, how her hair looks.
- Honor her request to wear a certain outfit.
- Look at her when she talks to me.
- Wear a cologne she loves.
- Let her know where I'm going and what I'm doing.
- Discuss spiritual themes together.
- Hug her in nonsexual ways—more than eight times a day.

3. Learn how to love sacrificially (if needed, review step four).

I,_____, commit to loving my wife and family by doing the following:

a. Becoming a servant. (List several ways to serve your wife and family.)

_____

_____

b. Continuing to support them financially. (What are your wife and family's financial needs?)

_____

_____

c. Providing additional help when needed. (What are several specific ways that you could provide other kinds of help for your wife?)

_____

_____

4. Initiate change in myself (if needed, review step five).

I,_____, commit to initiating change in the following areas of my life:

a. Mental. (List the specific things you can do to grow in this area.)

_____

_____

b. Physical. (List the specific things you can do to grow in this area.)

_____

_____

c. Spiritual. (List the specific things you can do to grow in this area.)

_____

_____

d. Social. (List the specific things you can do to grow in this area.)

_____

_____

5. Understand why your wife may not be in a position to reconcile at this time (if needed, review step six).

I, _____, commit to exploring and understanding the following reasons why my wife may not be ready to reconcile at this present moment:

a. Has your wife been the victim of emotional, physical, or sexual abuse (either by you or someone else)? Without using names, list the possible ways that your wife has been victimized in these areas. As you think about what she has been through, ask the Lord to give you understanding and wisdom in how you can best help your wife in this area.

_____

_____

b. Circle the personality that seems to fit your wife the best: lion, otter, golden retriever, or beaver. As a result of her personality, list several reasons why your wife may be resistant to your reconciliation. (You may need to review the section on personality types.)

_____

_____

c. As a result of your actions, are there any reasons why your wife's spirit is still closed?

_____

_____

You may need to repeat the following four steps in order to open her spirit:

a) Become soft and tender with my wife.
b) Gain a better understanding of what she has gone through.
c) Acknowledge any hurt, then admit my mistake and seek forgiveness.
d) Show genuine repentance.

6. Understand your ultimate goal in the reconciliation process (if needed, review step seven). What do the following passages tell you?

- James 5:16:

- Colossians 3:17:

- Psalm 112:

- Romans 5:3–5:

I, _____, commit to knowing God and letting Him become my strength. I will do the following specific things to seek after His ways:

7. I, _____, commit to learning what it means to be persistent in the reconciliation process.

Read Luke 18:1–8. What does this story have to do with your situation? What do you think God means by being persistent? What happens if you get a divorce? Does this mean you are to never give up on reconciliation? We encourage you to prayerfully and carefully consider these questions. Each situation and every individual is different. As a result, it is very important to think through questions like these in order to formulate your belief.

People around you will try to convince you that they have all the "right" answers. Be careful. You need to decide what you believe God is calling you to do in your situation. Even among Christians there is no agreement on how we should interpret what the Bible says about divorce and remarriage. In the book *Divorce and Remarriage*, Wayne House presents four perspectives on this difficult issue. We strongly encourage you to read his book to help you define your position more clearly.

8. Be responsible for your own accountability by joining a support group (if needed, review step nine).

I, _____, commit to joining a support group for the purpose of being held accountable to doing the things needed to bring about reconciliation with my wife and family.

List the names of some people whom you would like to hold you accountable:

1.
2.
3.
4.
5.
6.
7.
8.
9.
10.

By signing my name, I,_____, commit to following through with this plan for reconciliation. I also commit to being open to modifying my plan when changes are needed. But above learning to love my wife and children, I commit to becoming a man of God, no matter what happens in my marital relationship.

Your Signature:_____
Date:_____

Witness:_____
Date:_____
(A person who is going to hold you accountable)

Post Game
Interviews

Lord, Thank You for the Miracle!

W e've all enjoyed watching the spirited celebration
that erupts in the winners' locker room immediately
following a major sporting victory. Corks fly! Emotions soar!
The shouts of grown men whoopin' and hollerin' bounce off
the walls. Between the high fives and the champagne-
drenched hugs, the ever-present media maneuver to get their
postgame interviews.

In this book we have presented a game plan for reconciliation, briefly highlighting the relationship experiences of
Jack and Deanna, Dave, Mike, Jim and Jessica. Though their
marriage scoreboards posted different numbers, each
emerged a winner. They now find themselves enjoying the
dynamics of a winners' locker room.

They belong there because they beat the opposition.
They beat a defeated attitude, self-pity, guilt, and shame.
They resisted the temptation to blame. These couples were
victorious over the natural inclination to react in anger,
resentment, or bitterness. They refused to be bad sports.

Their stories beautifully illustrate God's game saver, Romans 8:28 (NKJV): "We know that all things work together for good to those who love God, to those who are the called according to His purpose." And their stories can be yours.

We managed to catch up with most of the players in this book and grabbed these quick, postgame interviews.

GARY: Deanna, you and Jack have successfully managed to keep your marriage together in spite of overwhelming odds. What does it feel like to now be enjoying this victory, with your husband at your side?

DEANNA: It has been a very difficult road, but I know God had, and still has, His hand on us. I feel blessed and honored to know God will help others by the victories we have had through Jesus.

GARY: Jack, as you stand here listening to your wife, what's going through your head?

JACK: I am so thankful God has blessed me with an incredible wife. It's truly because of her we are still together. My wife is the most beautiful woman in the world, inside and out.

GARY: Deanna, hearing praise like that must be icing on the cake.

DEANNA: I love Jack more today than I ever have.

GARY: Jack, how long has it been since that day you came clean?

JACK: It has been four years since that morning of confession. I'm very thankful to God for the victory He has given my family. It has been a hard-fought battle overcoming the personal foul I committed on my wife, but God is faithful. He has allowed me to win this game, and I know He will continue helping me through the play-offs of life—and into the Super Bowl—heaven!

GARY: What was the most important thing Jack did to save your marriage?

DEANNA: He had the guts to face the people he had betrayed: God, me, and the kids. Jack had to put his future, and his life, on the line. He took all his pride and ego and put that aside to make things right. Instead of continuing to live a lie, he openly told the truth.

GARY: How has that made a difference?

DEANNA: Telling the truth has set him free. He is now free to communicate openly to God and honestly to me.

GARY: You've obviously forgiven Jack for his infidelity. How were you able to do that?

DEANNA: I take no credit for all that I've been able to endure. The Lord has forgiven me, so how can I not forgive others? The most important thing is true forgiveness. When that happens, we can begin to trust again.

GARY: Jack, as you mounted your comeback drive, what one play proved most successful?

JACK: We got the most yardage from communication. You have to take time to talk—talk about the big things in life and the little things. I found that good communication is like throwing a long bomb for a completion.

GARY: What else worked for you?

JACK: Writing notes is something my wife really enjoys. This is an area I really need to work on. Another area is being accountable—to God, my wife, and other men. When I say something, I have to stick with it, to prove that my word is good. Reading the Bible and daily leading our family in quiet times have been very important.

GARY: Deanna, what relationship plays worked for you?

DEANNA: Seeing Jack on his knees before the Lord. Watching him give godly instruction to our children. It means a lot to me that he prays for me daily.

GARY: Any parting thoughts?

DEANNA: I admire Jack more than when we first got married. I also recognize that the enemy hates this idea of being faithful to our Lord and to each other. But God can see us through the darkest night and the strongest storm.

JACK: It was my sin, but we both had to pay the cost. Complete forgiveness from my wife seemed to take a long time, but actually, she forgave me quickly. It just took some time to regain her trust.

It has been more than ten years since Dave signed divorce papers. Since that time, his life has seen its share of highs and lows. But through it all, he has remained emotionally and spiritually anchored.

GARY: How have you dealt with the stigma that often accompanies having a failed marriage?

DAVE: I don't see myself as having been a failure. I was a fool. I was a fool because I didn't heed counsel on several fronts. I made foolish choices.

GARY: Foolish choices . . . divorce . . . So what qualifies you to now join these others in the winners' locker room?

DAVE: Because marriage is not the game; it's Jesus and the Christian life.

GARY: Many men are working to make their way from the defeated locker room into this victorious one. What one thing would you want to say to them?

DAVE: Actually, three things come to mind. First, God cares more about your spiritual growth than about saving your marriage. Second, concentrate on acquiring the qualities that were lacking that led to the demise of your relationship. Last, do not have a lady-in-waiting! Do not have someone in the wings just in case things don't work out with your wife. This person is a major distraction.

GARY: Perhaps this lady-in-waiting, as you call her, is a gift from God.

DAVE: I would consider her more a transition person. God will often put one or more women in your life for two specific reasons: (1) to give you an opportunity to practice new qualities, and (2) to give you an idea of what a relationship can be.

GARY: Did anything you learned from this whole ordeal surprise you?

DAVE: No, nothing really surprised me. I did discover that the attitudes that make for a successful marriage also make for a successful life.

GARY: That's good, and so important. What you're saying is, you think you're doing all these things for your wife, but you're actually doing it for your life! In the past ten-plus years since your divorce, you've remarried. How do you know remarriage was God's chosen plan for you and not a self-motivated pursuit to fill a void?

DAVE: Because there is safety in a multitude of counsel—and all the godly counsel I received said, "Marry her!"

GARY: Dave, how would you describe your life today?

DAVE: In a word, *joyful*. It's not always fun, but it is joyful and fulfilling.

Life is difficult. Sometimes it feels as if we're trying to bowl uphill! We expend a lot of energy, but rarely score. It takes deep commitment and unwavering persistence to hang in there. Persistence was Jim and Jessica's story—and it still is.

GARY: Jessica, how are things going with you and Jim?

JESSICA: We've been back together now for three years. What I have been witnessing lately is the strong pull of the world, the flesh, and the devil to again weaken our marriage.

GARY: How so?

JESSICA: Satan will attack even harder than before because he hates that God has restored our marriage. Spiritual warfare is definitely for real! The passion to grow spiritually that my husband had in the beginning has faded somewhat. Church attendance has slacked off. There's also been a kind of boredom that has set in. You get into a routine, and it isn't always a good routine. The spark that glowed bright in the beginning begins to fade a bit.

GARY: Jim, what would help to rekindle the flame?

JIM: Remembering why you fell in love with your wife in the first place. Keep the channels of communication open. Work side by side to put things back together. Have one common goal of putting the Lord first instead of myself.

GARY: You guys have really struggled with some serious issues. What have you learned along the way?

JIM: I've learned that it is very expensive in life to cheat on your mate. Purchasing one's ego with materialism and extramarital affairs is a very expensive price tag.

JESSICA: Christ must always be first. The minute my focus shifts away from that, I start to sink again. I need to daily strengthen my relationship with Christ so that I can be His daughter first and then the proper wife to Jim.

GARY: What can you say to other couples going through the same challenges?

JESSICA: Rely solely on Christ. Walk with Him step by step so you can go through the tragedy, not just put a Band-Aid on the situation. Consistent prayer, fellowship, and studying God's Word will defeat Satan.

GARY: Jessica, there are scores of men who have "fumbled away" possession of their marriage. What was Jim able to do to offset his numerous affairs? How could you take him back?

JESSICA: I saw his total humility, brokenness, and sincere remorse for his loose lifestyle. This softened my heart to let me forgive him and let him back into my life.

GARY: Do you have any advice you'd like to pass on?

JIM: If you are thinking about doing the same things I've done, reconsider. I also asked myself these questions: If I were broke, sick, or destitute, would this person be there for me? and Would I be there for her, given the same scenario?

GARY: Marrying the same person twice is not your usual scenario. What do you know this time around that you missed or weren't fully aware of the first time?

JESSICA: There are many things that I've come to realize and appreciate. For starters, never, never let down your guard regarding Satan's attacks! He is full of hate and does some of his ugliest work in marriages. He will always play on your fears of the past. Hold on tight, knowing that Christ has separated your sins as far as the east is from the west. Take each step with God, and you will find Satan under your feet. My marriage is far from problem free, but my foundation is Christ now. I rest in Him alone and am confident that "he who began a good work in you will carry it on to completion" (Phil 1:6 NIV).

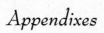

Appendixes

Appendix . . . .
A . . . .

Training Exercises

These are excellent for individual study or small group interaction.

1. Suppose you scored your marriage in terms of a football game. What is the score, and how much time is left in the game?

- Down by four touchdowns at half time.
- Down by a touchdown and into the two-minute drill.
- Down by a ton, with no timeouts; she has the ball.
- I don't know the score.

2. Let's say it's half time, and you're on the short end of a lopsided score. You're huddling with the guys in the locker room. What's your focus?

- Stop making stupid plays, turnovers, and penalties.
- Analyze why I have fallen behind.
- Get the ball back, and make several first downs.

- Listen to the Head Coach, and do the plays He calls.

3. If you are willing to do whatever it takes to win, but admit that until now you have not given it your best shot, which of the following have you not done consistently?

- Study the rule book (the Bible) and play by the rules.
- Understand the playbook (my wife).
- Obey the Head Coach (the Lord).
- Listen to others who coach and cheer me on.
- Get equipped with other resources.

4. To put together a balanced offense, you will want to enlist the help of the rule book (the Bible), the playbook (your wife), the Head Coach (God Himself), any assistant coaches you know (supporting ministries), scouts (counselors), and the other men in your huddle group. Spend some time identifying your behavior and attitudes that incur penalties, negative yardage, and loss of possession (turnovers). Of the following, what have you been flagged for in the past year? For which have you had repeated infractions?

- Illegal substitution—recruiting violations
- Intentionally grounding—playing the blame game
- Unsportsmanlike conduct—displaying a critical spirit
- False start—rushing her by your impatience
- Illegal snap—imposing a time frame for reconciliation
- Holding—prematurely initiating physical displays of affection
- Piling on—resorting to overkill in trying to do good
- Unnecessary roughness—underestimating hurt

- Offsides—disregarding boundaries

5. Suppose you are clueless about what happened in your troubled marriage. Invite others into your huddle to review the game films of your marriage up to the present. With 20/20 hindsight and instant replay, and in light of what you have learned in this book, what rules of the game do you now see that you violated?

———————————————————————————————

———————————————————————————————

6. The second half is about to begin and your Coach will put you back in the game only if you can clearly assess all the damage that your plays have caused the team. Look at the list under number 4 on page 160. Give yourself a penalty—5 yards for unintentional fouls, and 15 yards for intentional ones. Total up every one of the minus yards. How much ground have you lost in the first half of the game?

———————————————————————————————

———————————————————————————————

7. With the help of instant replay (any letters or messages from your wife), plus the encouragement of other men in your huddle group, try to identify the things you do that make first downs, gain positive yardage, keep possession of the reconciliation ball, and even score a few touchdowns. Next, which of the following behaviors typify you this past year?

- Giving thanks, even for my wife's wake-up call.
- Asking forgiveness and showing genuine repentance.
- Regarding my wife as the star QB calling the plays.

- Honoring my wife's boundaries, especially her "no."
- Loving my wife sacrificially, even when it hurts.
- Listening to her and learning from her built-in playbook.
- Contributing financially and helping in other areas.
- Showing tenderness, being vulnerable.
- Being in accountability relationships with others.
- Initiating change in myself—not her.

8. Review step five. Where have you gained the most yards? Where do you have the most room to improve—mentally, physically, spiritually, or socially?

_____

_____

9. Choose one aspect of your game to improve the next time you have the ball. What is that one aspect, and what specific changes do you plan on making?

_____

_____

10. Reflecting on your first few years of marriage, check which measure of each ingredient your wife would say you provided her.

Key: (*a*) not enough to survive, (*b*) enough to maintain the status quo, (*c*) enough to grow and flourish together

Sunlight: unconditional security (*a*)___ (*b*) ___ (*c*)___
Water: meaningful conversation (*a*) ___ (*b*) ___ (*c*) ___
Soil: emotional/romantic bonding (*a*) ___ (*b*) ___ (*c*) ___
Air: positive physical touching (*a*) ___ (*b*) ___ (*c*) ___

11. As you consider your relationship just prior to the separation or divorce, which ingredient(s) was particularly weak or absent?
- Sunlight
- Water
- Soil
- Air

12. Having identified that missing ingredient, list specific ways you can provide it for your wife, once you are given the opportunity.

_____

_____

13. The five things that women reported they valued most in a man make a fitting report card for husbands. Grade your effectiveness in each of these areas.

Key: A (the best), B, C, D, F (the worst)

____ A growing Christian and spiritual leader
____ A sense of humor and fun to be with
____ Integrity, honesty
____ Tenderness, gentleness, sensitivity
____ Prioritizes family

14. How many pieces of emotional baggage is your wife carrying around? Are they light or heavy? From what point of origin? Destination? Any lost items?

_____

_____

15. Which personality bent best describes your wife? With which animal do you most identify?

_____

_____

16. Read through the ten verses of Psalm 112. What do you sense is God's timely message for you?

_____

_____

17. You must understand the root cause of your marital problems. To help you toward that end, what would your wife say is the main reason you are not together right now?

_____

_____

18. Write down the things you did, but shouldn't have done, plus the things you should have done, but didn't.

_____

_____

19. Asking for help is difficult for many men, but the wise man asks. When was the last time you asked anyone for help? Whom do you know, trust, and respect enough to ask for significant help with what you are going through right now?

_____

_____

20. Pray for her (and you) to be relieved of deep-seated anger. The less anger on both your parts adds to her ability to receive your loving acts. If either you or your wife has too

much buried anger and/or bitterness, both will not be able to readily give or receive loving efforts. We gave you specific tools throughout this book to lessen anger levels.

_____

_____

21. You might consider doing a topical Bible study on patience, asking the Lord to cultivate His calm steadfastness in you. Remember the beautiful promise of Isaiah 26:3 (NKJV), "You will keep him in perfect peace, whose mind is stayed on You." You will need to trust the Lord on this one, and that's the posture He has wanted from you all along.

> Trust in the LORD with all your heart,
> And lean not on your own understanding;
> In all your ways acknowledge Him,
> And He shall direct your paths. (Prov. 3:5–6 NKJV)

Appendix . . . .
B: . . . .

Resources to Equip You

Rule book: the Bible
Playbook: your wife
Home field advantage: if you two live together
Huddle group: for support and accountability
Head coach: God

Assistant Coaches (Ministry Organizations)
- Smalley Relationship Center: call (800) 84-TODAY (to order books or videos) or (417) 335-4321 for seminar information (garysmalley.com).
- Promise Keepers: call (800) 456-PK94 (to order products) or (800) 888-PK95 (for men's conferences and information on small groups in your area).
- Focus on the Family: call (800) A-FAMILY.
- DivorceCare: call (800) 646-2001.
- Fresh Start: call (800) 882-2799.

Qualified Scouts (Counseling Centers)
- RAPHA Clinics: call (800) 383-4673.

Appendix B

- Larry Crabb & Associates: call (508) 977-5080.
- American Association of Christian Counselors: call (800) 526-8673.

Game Films (Video Series)
- *Hidden Keys to Loving Relationships*, eighteen thirty-minute videos by Gary Smalley
- *Love Is a Choice* (one video) by Drs. Minirth, Meier, and Hemfelt
- *Inside Out* (four videos) by Larry Crabb
- *Growing Closer: Building Christ-Centered Relationships* (three videos, six sessions) by Gail and Gordon MacDonald
- *DivorceCare* (fourteen videos) by Steve Grissom

Field Manuals (Books)
- Neil Anderson, *Breaking Through to Spiritual Maturity*
- Paul Billheimer, *Don't Waste Your Sorrows*
- Larry Crabb, *The Marriage Builder; Inside Out*
- Gordon Dalbey, *Healing the Masculine Soul; Fight Like a Man*
- James Dobson, *Straight Talk to Men and Their Wives; What Wives Wish Their Husbands Knew About Women*
- Tony Evans, *Returning to Your First Love*
- Bruce Fisher, *Rebuilding: When a Relationship Ends*
- Gene Getz, *The Measure of a Man*
- R. Kent Hughes, *Disciplines of a Godly Man*
- Jerry Jenkins, *Loving Your Marriage Enough to Protect It*
- Ann Jones and Susan Schecter, *When Love Goes Wrong: What to Do When You Can't Do Anything Right*

- Howard Markman and Scott Stanley, *Fighting for Your Marriage*
- Michael McManus, *Marriage Savers*
- Gary Oliver, *Real Men Have Feelings and How to Change Your Spouse Without Ruining Your Marriage*
- John Powell, *The Secret of Staying in Love*
- Promise Keepers, *Power of a Promise Kept; Seven Promises of a Promise Keeper; What Makes a Man?*
- Gary Rosberg, *Guard Your Heart*
- Gary Smalley, *Joy That Lasts; Hidden Keys of a Loving, Lasting Marriage*
- Gary Smalley and John Trent, *The Blessing; The Hidden Value of a Man; Love Is a Decision*
- John Trent, *Lifemapping*
- E. Glenn Wagner and Dietrich Gruen, *Strategies for a Successful Marriage*
- John White, *Eros Defiled*

Evaluation

Please help us with your comments about *Winning Your Wife Back*.

Fill out the following (*please print*):

Age: 18–30_____ 31–40_____ 41–50_____ 51–Above_____

Presently Married_____ Separated_____ Divorced_____
If so, when?_____

Second Marriage?_____
Did you receive marriage counseling?_____

Did you receive any premarital counseling?_____
How many sessions?___

Occupation_____ Children_____
If so, give ages_____

Evaluation

How would you rate the book from 1 to 10? (1=poor, 10=excellent)___

What benefited you the most from the book?_____
_____
_____
_____

What would you change to improve the book?_____
_____
_____
_____

What other topics should be addressed in a book like this?_____
_____

If you have a testimony or story you would like to share with us that could possibly help us understand or help others in future versions, use this space:

_____
_____
_____
_____
_____
_____
_____
_____
_____

Mail to: Smalley Relationship Center, 1482 Lakeshore Drive, Branson, MO 65616. If your story is used all names and identifying details will be changed.

Notes

Pregame Warm-Up
Lord, I Need a Miracle!

1. Michelle Weiner-Davis, *Divorce Busting* (New York: Simon and Shuster Inc.,1992), 102.

Step One
Understand How "Penalty Flags" Can Damage the Reconciliation Process

1. John Wooden, *They Call Me Coach* (Waco: Word Publishers,1972), 123.
2. Gary Smalley, *Hidden Keys to Loving Relationship Workbook* (Paoli: Relationships Today, 1998), 23.
3. Smalley, *Hidden Keys to Loving Relationship Workbook*, 25.
4. Howard Markman, Scott Stanley, and Susan Blumberg, *Fighting for Your Marriage* (San Fransisco: Jossey-Bass, 1994), 18.

Step Two
Open a Closed Spirit

1. G. Smalley, *Hidden Keys to Loving Relationships Workbook*, 32.
2. G. Smalley, *Hidden Keys to Loving Relationships Workbook*, 33.
3. NOTE: There may be unresolved issues in your life that impede you from being the listener you could be. An assistant coach (counselor) may prove beneficial for you.
4. See penalty flag "Recruiting."
5. Peter Kreeft, *Making Choices* (Michigan: Ann Arbor, 1990), 197–98.

Step Three
Honor Your Wife and Children

1. See penalty flag, "Disregarding Boundaries."

Step Four
Develop Sacrificial Love

1. Ed Mack Miller, "The Man Who Matched Our Mountains" *Denver Post*, December 3, 1961.
2. John Wooden, *They Call Me Coach* (Waco: Word Publishers,1972), cover copy.

Step Five
Initiate Change in Yourself

1. If an affair (emotional or physical) has been present within your marital relationship, we strongly encourage you to read Dave Carder's book, *Torn Asunder: Recovering*

from Extramarital Affairs. Dave offers practical how-to's to bring about healing.

Step Six
Understand Why Some Women Are Not in a Position to Reconcile

1. See penalty flags " Being Impatient" and "Setting a Time Frame."
2. The Personal Strengths Survey and Chart were adapted from Gary Smalley and John Trent's book, *The Two Sides of Love*, 34–35.
3. Refer to step two to review how to open a closed spirit.

Step Seven
Understand the Ultimate Goal When Your Wife Leaves

1. Once again, because of the deep pain of marital separation, let me encourage you to consider reading a book I wrote several years ago called *Joy That Lasts*. In it I explain how the Lord reached down and picked me up as I traveled through a very hurtful circumstance—something like a divorce. I address the important areas of ridding ourselves of anger and hurt, in addition to addressing how to turn difficult situations and trials into good for us and glory for the Lord.

Step Eight
Never Give Up!

1. Gary Smalley, *Joy That Lasts* (Grand Rapids, MI: Zondervan, 1986), 49.

2. Churchill, as quoted in John Bartlett, *Familiar Quotations* 15th ed. (Boston, Little, Brown, 1980).

Step Nine
Be Accountable by Joining a Support Group

1. Gary Smalley and John Trent, *The Hidden Value of a Man*, (Colorado Springs: Focus on the Family Publishing, 1992) 136–51.
2. Rod Handley, *Character Counts—Who's Counting Yours* (Grand Island, NE: Cross Training Publishing, 1945).

Step Ten
Understand Women: The Scouting Report

1 Allen P. Ross, *Creation and Blessing* (Grand Rapids, MI.: Baker Book House, 1988), 126.
2. John Powell, *The Secret of Staying in Love* (Niles: Argus Communications 1974), 70.
3. We encourage you to review the "drive-through listening" method of communication. This method is specifically designed to help a man learn how to listen to and understand his wife.
4. The man who just can't keep his hands off her is referred to the penalty sections, "Displaying Affection in Physical Ways" and "Disregarding Boundaries."

To receive a free catalog of information, to order books, videotapes, or cassettes, or to receive an updated seminar schedule by Gary Smalley, write:

Smalley Relationship Center
1482 Lakeshore Drive
Branson, Missouri 65616
Call toll free: 1-800-848-6329
www.garysmalley.com

Books:
Making Love Last Forever
Making Love Last Forever Curriculum Series
If Only He Knew
For Better or For Best
Joy That Lasts
Hidden Keys of a Loving, Lasting Marriage
The Two Sides of Love
The Language of Love
Love Is a Decision
The Hidden Value of a Man
The Gift of the Blessing
Leaving the Light On
The Key to Your Child's Heart
The Treasure Tree
Home Remedies

Videotapes:
Hidden Keys to Loving Relationships
Homes of Honor Relationship Small Group Series
(I and II)

Homes of Honor Parenting Small Group Series

Cassettes:
"Love Is a Decision" Seminar Series
"The Keys to Your Child's Heart Book Trax"
"Love Is a Decision Book Trax"
"The Hidden Value of a Man Book Trax"

GARY SMALLEY is one of the country's best-known authors and speakers on family relationships. He is the author of sixteen best-selling, award-winning books along with several popular films and videos. He is a frequent guest on national radio programs such as *Focus on the Family with Dr. James Dobson* and has made television appearances on *Oprah*, CNN productions including *Larry King Live*, NBC's *Today*, and *The 700 Club*. He has also reached hundreds of thousands through his Love Is a Decision seminars, as well as through Promise Keepers events.

DR. GREG SMALLEY graduated with his doctorate degree in clinical psychology from Rosemead School of Psychology at Biola University in Southern California. He also holds master's degrees in counseling psychology (Denver Seminary) and clinical psychology (Rosemead). Dr. Smalley is the director of research and development at Smalley Relationship Center in Branson, Missouri. He lives in Ozark, Missouri, with his wife, Erin, and their two daughters, Taylor and Madalyn.

DEBORAH SMALLEY, a graduate of the University of California at Long Beach, is the founder of Faith Lift! Ministries in Orange, California. Her mission is to encourage, exhort, and equip Christians to live God-honoring lives; she does this through speaking, writing, and music. Deborah spent countless hours researching, interviewing, and writing *Winning Your Wife Back Before It's Too Late*. She lives in Santa Ana, California.